Improving Your Garden Soil

Created and designed by
the editorial staff of
ORTHO BOOKS

Project Editor
Barbara J. Braasch

Writer
Barbara Perry Lawton

Photography Editor
Roberta Spieckerman

Illustrator
Paul Kratter

Designer
Gary Hespenheide

Ortho Books

Publisher
Richard E. Pile, Jr.

Editorial Director
Christine Jordan

Production Director
Ernie S. Tasaki

Managing Editors
Robert J. Beckstrom
Michael D. Smith
Sally W. Smith

System Manager
Linda M. Bouchard

Marketing Specialist
Daniel Stage

Sales Manager
Thomas J. Leahy

Distribution Specialist
Barbara F. Steadham

Technical Consultant
J. A. Crozier, Jr., Ph.D.

Address all inquiries to:
Ortho Books
Chevron Chemical Company
Consumer Products Division
Box 5047
San Ramon, CA 94583

Chevron Chemical Company
6001 Bollinger Canyon Road
San Ramon, CA 94583

Acknowledgments

Soils Consultant
William E. Chaney

Copy Chief
Melinda E. Levine

Editorial Coordinator
Cass Dempsey

Copyeditor
Barbara Feller-Roth

Proofreader
Deborah Bruner

Indexer
Trisha Feuerstein

Layout by
Cynthia Putnam

Composition by
Laurie A. Steele

Associate Editor
Sara Shopkow

Production by
Studio 165

Separations by
Color Tech. Corp.

Lithographed in the USA by
Webcrafters, Inc.

Special Thanks to
Brooklyn Botanic Garden, Chicago Botanic Garden, Golden Gate Park, the Merchant family, Missouri Botanical Garden Library, the Nadler family, Kenneth Peck, Jim Wilson, and the many extension agents of the United States Extension Service who shared their knowledge generously.

Landscape Designers/Nurseries
Jim Hanson Landscape Design; Martinez, Calif.: 54–55
Sequoya Nursery; Oakland, Calif.: 32–33
Smith & Hawken; Mill Valley, Calif.: front cover
Really Special Plants and Gardens; Berkeley, Calif.: 32–33

Photography Assistant
Karen Heilman

Photographers
Names of photographers are followed by the page numbers on which their work appears. R=right, C=center, L=left, T=top, B=bottom.

Liz Ball: 15T, 23T, 30, 43, 53, 75, 89, 95T
Laurie Black: 86, 101
John Blaustein: 29
Margarite Bradley, Positive Images: 22
Karen Bussolini, Positive Images: 39B, 88B
David Cavagnaro: 9BL, 63B, back cover TR
Chicago Botanical Gardens: 27TR
Josephine Coatsworth: 98, 100T
Karen Heilman: 49B
Saxon Holt: front cover, 23B, 32–33, 54–55, 65, 66, 68, 78, 80–81
Jerry Howard, Positive Images: 14T, 28, 37, 44, 45, 47, 52, 59, 70, 82, 84, 90R, back cover TL & BL
Betsy Kissam, Brooklyn Botanical Gardens: 27TL
Robert Kourik: 16T, 34
Michael Landis: 1, 6, 10, 12BL, 42, 48, 51 (all), 56, 57, 64, 67
Elvin McDonald: 38, 39T, 49T, 58, 60, 61, 100B
Michael McKinley: 25, 85, 88T, 99
James McNair: 9T, 24
Charles Mann: 4–5, 87T, 90L, 93, 105
Ortho Library: 9BR, 16B, 41, 46, 63T, 83, 92, 94, 95B, 97T, back cover BR
San Francisco Parks and Recreation: 27B
Tom Tracy: 31, 87B
Wolf von dem Bussche: 97B

Front Cover
Soil enriched with regular additions of organic matter is easy to cultivate and highly productive.

Back Cover
Top left: Adding amendments to soil is the best way to improve its structure and texture.

Top right: The gardener has bought earthworms to aerate the soil naturally and improve its water movement.

Bottom left: When soil is on the acid side, gardeners may want to add lime to raise the pH level.

Bottom right: Used as a mulch for seedlings, black plastic film warms the soil and deters weed germination.

Title Page
Planting vegetables in furrows is particularly beneficial in saline soils. If enough water is applied, it moves freely through the soil, carrying salts beyond the plant's root zone.

Improving Your Garden Soil

Keys to Good Soil

Achieving an ideal garden can be as simple as making the soil match plant requirements. Improving any soil virtually guarantees a more beautiful and productive garden.

Millions of green-thumbers have discovered the joy of gardening, surely one of the best ways to tune into the world of nature. It's hard to think of another hobby that combines healthy exercise with such tangible results. But if your garden doesn't thrive, if vegetables don't produce and flowers don't bloom, then gardening becomes a frustrating avocation.

Beneath every successful garden is a hidden hero—its soil. Once gardeners understand this basic fact, they have taken a giant step toward learning how to begin with a bare patch of ground and end up with lush ornamentals and bountiful vegetables and fruits.

Why is soil so important? Quite simply, in addition to providing physical support for plants, it conducts air, water, and nutrients to their root systems. Soil is the underground environment that influences plant growth. Whether you're starting from scratch or smarting from failure to achieve a dream crop the first time around, this book assures a greater chance of success in future projects.

Gardening is both an art and a science. The art lies in the choice of plants and the design of their placement. Garden science includes learning what plants need and how to provide the correct soil environment by supplying the necessary nutrients and moisture. This chapter

No matter how grand or small a garden, its success depends on how well the soil supplies what the plants need for good growth.

If a handful of soil falls apart after being squeezed, it's dry enough to be spaded or tilled easily.

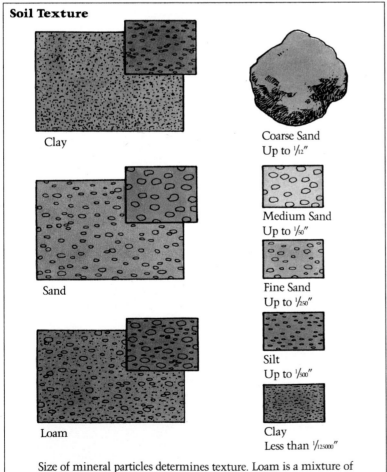

Soil Texture

Clay

Sand

Loam

Coarse Sand
Up to $1/12''$

Medium Sand
Up to $1/60''$

Fine Sand
Up to $1/250''$

Silt
Up to $1/500''$

Clay
Less than $1/125000''$

Size of mineral particles determines texture. Loam is a mixture of sand and clay.

delves into that science, identifies problems, and explains how to analyze a particular plot of ground and test its soil. Future chapters suggest ways to deal with less than ideal underground environments.

Soil preparation makes the difference between mediocrity and excellence in any garden. Without appropriate soil assessment and improvement, plants may not thrive and, indeed, may not survive. Heed the advice given by any good nursery and garden center: "Prepare your soil!" This book shows you how.

SOIL SCIENCE—A SHORT COURSE

Before soil can be improved, it's important to understand just what it is and how it contributes to plant growth. Soil science is a complex and often highly technical subject. But most gardeners will tell you that it's important to have at least a passing acquaintance with such basics as soil texture, structure, depth, and chemical composition.

Basically, soil is made up of varying sizes of mineral and organic particles mixed with quantities of air and water. Proportions may vary but the basic recipe remains the same. The mineral elements come from the weathered rocks that make up the earth's crust, the organic matter from decaying remains of plants and animals.

Soil Texture

The size of the mineral particles in soil creates its texture and defines its type. The three basic types of particles (in order of increasing size) are clay, silt, and sand. Clay and sand are also the names of two soil textures; loam, the most desirable of garden soils, includes all three particle types.

There's a simple test to determine soil texture. Moisten the soil and rub some between your thumb and fingers to determine its "feel." Sands are harsh and gritty and will scarcely hold together; clay can be squeezed into a firm shape. Silty sands can be somewhat gritty, too, but they cling together better when moist.

Classifying a soil by texture helps gardeners determine water and air circulation and water retention properties. It also gives a clue as to how easy it will be to till the soil.

Particles of clay are so small that most of them are not visible under a microscope. And because of their extremely small size they have a tendency to pack and become dense, shutting out air and water. At the other extreme, sandy soils usually contain much soil air, and drain—and dry out—quickly.

Loam soils contain approximately 10 to 20 percent clay, 25 to 70 percent silt, and 20 to 65 percent sand. The best loams for gardening are those that also include substantial amounts of humus (partly decomposed organic material), which helps the sandy soils retain moisture and nutrients and opens up the clay soils for air and water penetration.

Soils are seldom 100 percent clay, silt, or sand. To properly describe their consistency, scientists developed the soil texture triangle shown on page 19. It classifies soil according to the percentages of the minerals found in it. For example, if your soil is about 15 percent clay, 65 percent sand, and 20 percent silt, it would be classified as sandy loam.

Soil Structure

Optimum soils need good structure as well as texture. Texture refers to the proportions of sand, silt, and clay in soil particles; structure is the way those soil particles are held together. Knowing how particles are arranged in different types of soil explains how easily water, air, and nutrients can circulate through them and how well the soil will hold moisture and nutrients.

Soil particles collect naturally into relatively stable granules called aggregates, or peds. These aggregates come in a variety of shapes, sizes, and cohesive strengths. They may be stuck together by organic matter or by a variety of other substances, such as carbonates, iron oxides, clays, and silica.

Some aggregates, such as clay, are columnar, with comparatively long vertical dimensions. Others are platelike and more horizontal. This latter type is associated with compacted and hardpan soils, both of which are very hostile to plant root growth.

Rounded and blocky aggregates, typical of desirable loamy soils, are heaped together like piles of children's building blocks, with plenty of space between the granules for movement of air and water to foster plant root growth.

Working moist organic matter into the soil will help improve its structure. As plants decompose naturally, their dead leaves, stems, and roots also make valuable additions.

Soil Structure

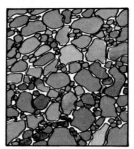

Compacted Soil
Packed particles leave little space for air or water

Crumbly Soil
Cultivating soil and adding organic matter turn aggregates into porous crumbs

Saturated Soil
Plants may drown if water cannot drain through the soil

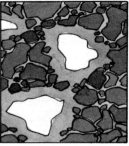

Moist Soil
A film of water between soil particles, and air in all but the small pores, mean soil is well drained

Soil Particles

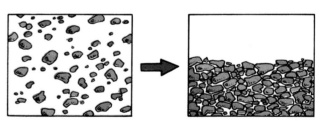

Compacted Soil
Individual, nonaggregated particles pack into a solid mass with no space for air or water

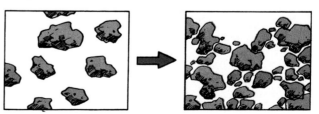

Crumbly Soil
Cultivation and soil amendments aggregate particles into porous granules

Soil Depth

If given a choice, most plants prefer a deep, well-drained topsoil with both good texture and structure. Deep soils hold more moisture and more nutrients than shallow soils with similar structure.

The depth of a soil is measured by how far below the surface plant roots can extend before being stopped by barriers, such as rock, sand, gravel, heavy clay, compacted dirt, or cement. Below the topsoil (usually only a few inches deep) lies another layer called subsoil. Usually more dense than topsoil and containing less organic matter, this 24- to 36-inch-deep band serves as both a water and nutrient reservoir for plants.

Even the largest trees can grow successfully in 36 to 60 inches of topsoil and subsoil. Conversely, shallow soils less than 10 inches deep are suitable only for shallow-rooted plants: most annuals, some alpines, and perennials.

How deep is your soil? To check, simply dig a hole. If you encounter an impenetrable layer in the first two feet, the soil may not be deep enough to support all the plants you are planning to grow.

Chemical Makeup

Since plants obtain most of their food from the soil, certain elements must be present in usable form if the plants are to thrive. If these elements are missing, then they must be added to the soil in the form of fertilizers. Soil tests, described later in this chapter, can help point the way toward correcting any possible soil deficiencies.

Plants need a number of different elements to grow normally. Carbon, hydrogen, and oxygen from air and water plus nitrogen from the soil make up 95 percent of plant solids. Nitrogen is the one element usually lacking in garden soil, since most plants can't take it directly from the atmosphere. They need a form of soluble salts called nitrates. (Legumes, an exception, have special root nodules where bacteria convert the nitrogen.)

Other elements often added to soils through fertilizing include calcium, magnesium, phosphorus, and potassium. Soils usually contain enough iron, copper, sulfur, manganese, zinc, boron, chlorine, cobalt, and molybdenum to meet plant needs. The pH factor of the soils (balance between acid and alkali) affects the availability of essential elements, and can have a detrimental effect on plant health. Ways to change soil pH are described on page 43.

Soil Organisms

Many gardeners know little about the living community of microbes that exists in healthy soils. But the knowledgeable ones tip their hats to these hardworking soil organisms by mulching and keeping soil moist to support and encourage the beneficial underground population.

Some organisms appear to have little or no effect on gardening soils; others can carry diseases harmful to plants. Many of these tiny organisms, however, perform vital roles in decomposing organic material and converting atmospheric nitrogen into nitrates. Also, they may be directly beneficial to plant growth processes in ways not yet thoroughly understood.

Microscopic soil dwellers include fungi (members of a plant group noted for lack of chlorophyll) that live on decaying animal and plant matter, bacteria (typically single-celled

Root Depth

Carrot   Azalea   Tomato   Tulip

Topsoil

Subsoil

Shallow-rooted plants such as most annuals and some perennials can grow in soils less than 10″ deep

Top: These short-season vegetable plants need a continuous and uniform supply of nutrients for proper growth. Bottom: Tomatoes benefit from the addition of soil-aerating earthworms (left), but the cutworm (right) can level seedlings.

With fertile, well-watered soil and plenty of sun, tomato plants flourish in patio containers.

organisms) that live on fungi and the surface of soil particles, and protozoan (single-celled animals). Soils are also home to larger organisms: grubs, earthworms, rodents, snakes, and other animal and plant forms. Larger animals such as the earthworm, which aerates the soil, are assets to the garden; other animals may be pests.

HOW YOUR GARDEN GROWS

A garden soil's role in plant growth is to supply nutrients, water, and air and provide a firm foundation for the root system. To carry out this assignment satisfactorily, most garden soils need some improvement.

Plant roots are demanding. They need support and space to anchor the plant in the ground without physical obstacles to block them. They also require an ample supply of moisture and nutrients to sustain the plant's health and promote the growth of new leaves, flowers, and fruits.

Plants will grow in less than ideal soil, but to give them the best chance it's important to create the most hospitable environment possible. An ideal gardening soil contains 2 to 5 percent organic matter, 45 to 48 percent mineral matter, 25 percent water, and 25 percent air.

Fertility alone won't guarantee a productive garden. Other considerations, such as the soil characteristics mentioned previously, drainage conditions, and, in some areas, erosion, slope, or rocky ground, may influence gardening success. Soil temperature is also a major factor in plant growth. If it is not within the required range for the plant, roots won't grow, no matter how healthy the soil.

Photosynthesis

Although this book is about the relationship between soils and plants, it helps to know a little about photosynthesis, the process by which green plants are able to manufacture their own food through their leaves. With adequate sunlight, plants can convert the water and carbon dioxide in its green cells into carbohydrates (sugars) and oxygen.

Sunlight is absorbed by the green material in leaves called chlorophyll. It's this chlorophyll within the plant cells that makes it possible for the plant to change the carbon dioxide from the air and water from the soil.

Anything that interferes with photosynthesis can harm the plant, since it needs carbohydrates to flourish. Without an adequate supply, its growth is poor or slow.

During the photosynthesis process, plants require large quantities of water for best response. The water is drawn up into the leaves through the plant's roots and stems. The water moistens the cells and minute breathing pores of the leaves, protecting them from dehydration.

Photosynthesis

With adequate
sunlight, plants
produce food through
their leaves and release
water and oxygen

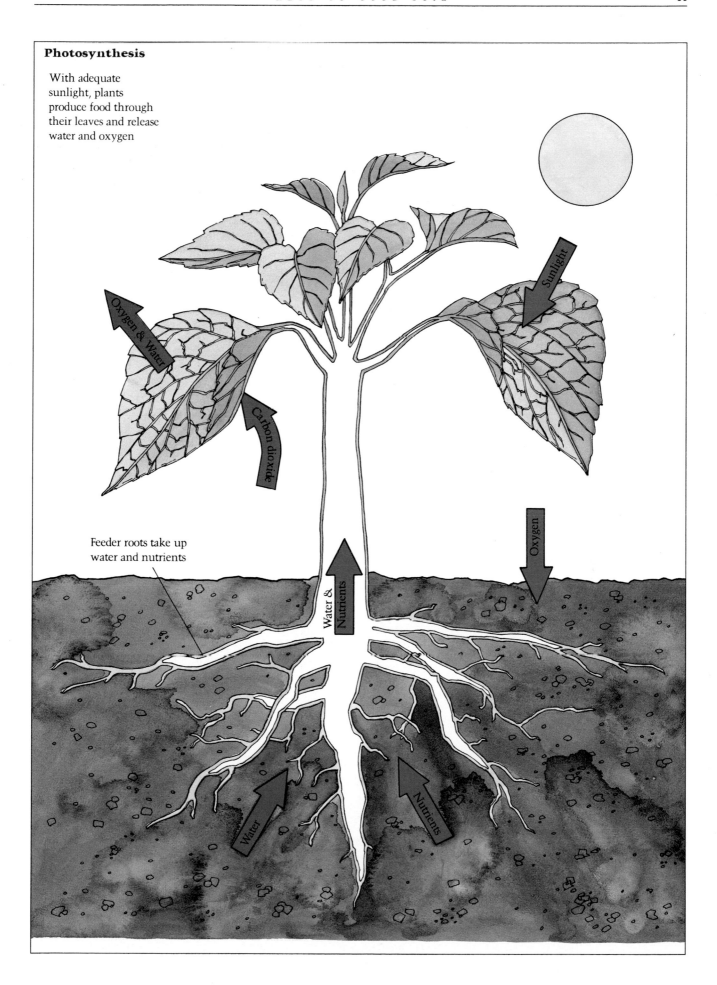

Feeder roots take up
water and nutrients

Soil Nutrients

The most abundant elements in plant tissues are carbon, hydrogen, and oxygen, all of which plants get largely from carbon dioxide and water. Plants also require relatively large amounts of nitrogen, phosphorus, and potassium, elements (often referred to as macronutrients) that usually have to be added to the soil in the form of fertilizers.

Calcium, magnesium, and sulfur are generally present in soils in sufficient amounts or added coincidentally with other elements. The traces of other elements required for plant growth, called micronutrients, are also found in the soil or added with other elements.

If plants lack nutrients, they may develop disturbing symptoms such as those discussed on page 13.

Soil Moisture

Water is found in the gaps between soil particles and is also held, or adsorbed, to the surfaces of clay, silt, and organic particles. The irregularly shaped soil particles create similarly shaped gaps which form an interconnected system of channels in the soil.

The exact amount of moisture in the soil varies with rain, irrigation, and general weather conditions, including heat, humidity, and wind speed. Soils also hold water with differing intensity. Those with high percentages of clay or organic matter cling tightly to moisture because of their greater adsorptive qualities. Sand allows water to escape with ease, since its particles adsorb little moisture.

Water moves upward through soils by capillary action. When surface water evaporates, water from deeper in the soil is sucked up to the surface because of pressure differences. It drains down due to gravity.

Air in Soil

If soils are compacted or too wet, plants and the organisms that live below the ground are often deprived of the air they require. Well-aerated soils are essential for the health of most plants.

The rates of oxygen consumed and carbon dioxide produced by plant roots vary according to soil temperature and moisture. Usually, aeration is not a problem as long as good soil texture and structure are maintained.

Soil Support

The larger the plant, the more important its roots as anchors in the soil. How much space does a root system need? Obviously, trees require a far wider and deeper field for their support than do annuals in garden borders.

Created as a private oasis, this sunny garden grows in containers on a rooftop high above busy city streets. Larger plants might require staking.

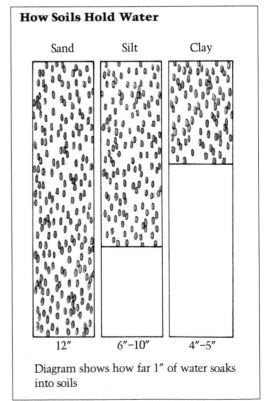

How Soils Hold Water

Sand   Silt   Clay

12″   6″–10″   4″–5″

Diagram shows how far 1″ of water soaks into soils

Reading Plant Health

Before blaming plant problems on nutrient deficiencies, gardeners will want to run through a mental checklist of environmental conditions that could affect growing conditions. Is the plant receiving sufficient light and the right amounts of water and air in the soil and atmosphere? Are day and night temperature readings within the required range?

Although many plants are able to adapt to a variety of environments, when they are moved from one location to a drastically different one, they may develop temporary symptoms of poor health. The first chart offers tips to reading plant health based on environment; the second explains symptoms of nutrient deficiency.

Testing is the only sure way to find out what nutrients are available in garden soils. Good gardeners analyze and correct their soils before plants show symptoms.

Environmental Factor	Symptoms
Too much water	Wilted foliage, rotting roots, older leaves begin to drop.
Too little water	Wilted foliage, younger leaves drop first.
Too much light	Foliage pales, may appear seared.
Too little light	Growth becomes leggy, spindly; plants reach for light.
Too much heat	Wilted foliage, growth stops.
Too much cold	Wilted foliage, roots rot.

Nutrient	Role in Plant Growth	Deficiency Symptoms
Nitrogen (N)	Stimulates vegetative growth.	Leaves are small, pale; old ones may begin to drop. Growth is thin and spindly. Symptoms appear first on lower leaves and work upward.
Phosphorus (P)	Root development. Important to seed germination, seedling development, ripening of fruits and seeds.	Color generally dull with tints of bronze and red; may appear scorched. Growth is stunted.
Potassium (K)	Root development, general vigor, disease resistance.	Squatty, stunted growth. Starting with their margins, older leaves may yellow, scorch, and die; edges may roll up.
Calcium (Ca)	Development of root system and growing points (meristems). Important part of cell walls in plant tissue.	Terminal buds die, blossoms may have black heart, roots are poorly developed, young foliage may turn yellow. Leaves become distorted with hooked tips, marginal scorching.
Magnesium (Mg)	Vital for chlorophyll production.	Leaves yellow between veins. Defoliation may become severe. Shows first on older leaves.
Sulfur (S)	Necessary for chlorophyll production. A component of proteins.	Young growth is restricted. Leaves turn yellow and become brittle; small leaves roll toward upper surface. Defoliation becomes severe, terminal buds die.
Iron (Fe)	Respiration and other oxidation processes, important for chlorophyll production.	Leaves yellow between veins, possibly followed by leaves turning almost white. Leaf margins may scorch.
Manganese (Mn)	Involved in chlorophyll production, catalyst in enzyme systems.	Foliage yellows between veins, with older foliage affected first. Leaves may crinkle and become cupped.
Boron (B)	Cell water regulator, necessary for translocation of sugars, important to reproduction.	Growing ends thicken and die, often forming distorted form called witches'-broom. Fruit also becomes deformed.
Zinc (Zn)	Important to maturity and size of plant, necessary for protein synthesis.	Foliage yellows between veins. Leaves, small and narrow, form rosettelike growth.
Copper (Cu)	Reproductive growth, necessary for protein synthesis.	Younger leaves yellow between veins, become thick and crinkled. Leaves are small; shoots die back.
Molybdenum (Mo)	Necessary to nitrogen processing.	Chlorosis, mottling and dieback of leaves. Growth stunted.
Chlorine (Cl)	Regulator of tissue water pressures, may affect maturity and influence photosynthesis.	

Note: Plants require only traces of such micronutrients as boron, zinc, copper, molybdenum, and chlorine; deficiencies are uncommon.

Sturdy black-eyed-susans and a colorful array of other splashy ornamentals thrive in full sun.

Root Support

Soil serves as a plant anchor, yet even a tree's feeder roots lie only 6″–8″ below the surface

It was once thought that the roots and tops of woody plants, trees, and shrubs needed the same reach and shape below ground as they did above. Today, we know that most plant roots, especially small feeder roots, are found in the top six to eight inches of soil.

Staking might be needed to support large plants until they are established and new roots have a chance to grow. All young trees used to be staked as a common practice, but current thinking is that the stress of resisting winds causes the tree to develop much stronger anchoring roots.

Soil Temperature

Light, temperature, and water are tightly woven environmental factors that govern plant development. How a plot of ground is oriented to the sun, therefore, affects the success of the garden. South-facing slopes are warmer than those facing north, for example.

Because soil temperature depends on sunlight, it fluctuates according to season and climate. Even the color of soil affects absorption of sunlight, with dark soils being warmer than light ones. And soils shaded by lush plantings are cooler than those open to the sun's rays.

Soil temperatures also vary according to the rate of moisture evaporation. Damp soils retain heat longer. One of the main reasons for adding

In their natural environment, ferns and other woodland plants prefer moist, sun-screened settings.

mulches to soil surfaces is to control the amount of heat the soil receives as well as the rate of heat dissipation.

Problem Plantings

Solving gardening problems is a little bit like working a puzzle. You have to search for the right clues before you can discover the possible answers.

When plants are not growing as they should, careful observation can help uncover the reason. Although some problems can be traced directly to soil deficiencies, other factors must be eliminated before positively identifying soil as the culprit.

Is the problem plant one that would normally thrive in this garden with this particular climate and exposure? Could the problem be caused by physical damage from pests or from disease? You can find answers to such questions by contacting state university extension experts (see page 108) and knowledgeable staff at botanical gardens, plant nurseries, and gardening centers.

Many garden problems can be traced simply to placing the wrong plant in the wrong place. Most plants are fairly tolerant of a wide range of soils and exposures, but some are particular, needing special growing conditions. As almost everyone knows, for instance, azaleas respond

Site Orientation

Soil temperatures vary depending on the amount and intensity of sunlight. South-facing soils accumulate heat and encourage rapid plant growth.

A construction cut exposes soil layers. The dark brown band under the surface is topsoil; subsoil colors range from orange to tan.

best in acid soils, and shade-loving plants droop and wilt in full sun. That's why it's important to learn what a plant requires before you buy it.

INTERPRETING THE LANDSCAPE

By the very nature of their composition, soils constantly change. And, although all types of soil are composed of mineral and organic material, water, and air, their proportions vary widely. These volume variations are responsible for many differences in soils.

Soils differ widely throughout the country and even within a small area. These soil differences are due to the types of rock from which the soils came and also to the length of weathering time.

One valuable guide to regional soils is the map published by the U. S. Soil Conservation Service (see page 103). Among other things, it reveals that New England and much of Florida have acid soils caused by losing soluble,

Native plants that require little water are the best choices for Southwest gardens.

alkaline nutrients through leaching by rainfall. By contrast, in the arid Southwest, soils are typically saline and alkaline.

Horizons and Profiles

Most soils consist of three main vertical layers called horizons, one above the other, with different colors and other properties. The horizons are produced by the longtime effects of climate and vegetation on mineral matter. Collectively, these horizons make up a soil profile.

Uncovering these hidden depths helps gardeners decide what type of plants can be grown in their areas. You don't have to see all the layers to have a good garden, but taking a look increases knowledge of soil makeup. Highway cuts and nearby residential construction sites are good places to find exposed soil layers.

If you dig through the lower layers of soil and find no definite bands, it's reasonable to assume that the soil has been moved around and mixed up recently. Some good examples include man-made landfills, soils that have been deposited in floodplains along streams, and newly formed sand dunes.

Colors

Soil comes in a rainbow of hues, from chalky white through yellow, orange, and brown to nearly black. The color of soil is determined by its mineral and organic makeup, its drainage condition, and the degree of oxidation or extent of weathering.

Light-colored surface soils are low in organic matter and often coarse in texture. Pale soils frequently are highly leached, meaning that many of their nutrients have been washed away by water over the years. These light soils are often found in areas with high average temperatures.

A dark soil color can indicate a high organic content or it may mean poor drainage, low average temperatures, or other causes of slow oxidation of organic matter.

Soil Profile

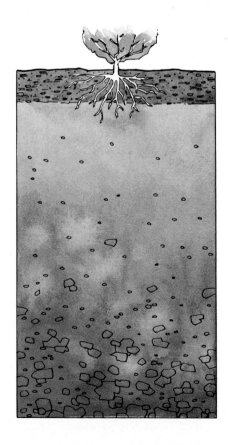

Topsoil

The first soil horizon is the topsoil, which is generally 4 to 6 inches thick. More fertile than underlying soils, topsoil is more enriched with organic matter than the layers beneath it. This is the soil layer that most concerns gardeners, since it's the bed for plants. When soil improvement is mentioned, the topsoil and the subsoil (see below) are the ones to be amended.

Subsoil

The horizon under the topsoil is called the subsoil and may reach a depth of 30 inches. It's finer and more even textured than topsoil; it's also more compact, partly because it contains less organic matter. Subsoil supports surface soil and stores water and nutrients leached from the topsoil.

When exposed during construction, subsoil must be incorporated into a garden. If too compact, it can inhibit root and water penetration. Ways to amend its texture and increase its fertility are described in the next chapter.

Bottom Soil

The deepest soil layer consists of decomposed rock, parent material that has characteristics of the subsoil above it and the bedrock beneath it. This parent soil is mostly responsible for the texture, natural fertility, rate of formation, acidity, and depth of the soil horizons above.

Mineral content affects subsoil colors, turning them yellow, red, or brown. Topsoil can also reflect its mineral makeup; a high iron content, for example, results in red soil.

Lay of the Land

Creating soil from solid rock is a continual process involving a combination of factors, including climate, plant and animal organisms, the type of parent rock, and the land's topography. Two powerful influences are those notorious transporters of soil—wind and water.

The surrounding landscape provides clues as to soil type: Hilltop soil is usually far more shallow than valley soil; prairie topsoil will probably be deep and fertile. In contrast, topsoil is normally very thin in the desert and only moderately thick under the humid, forested regions.

The lay of the land tells a lot about its drainage, too. Low-lying areas receive water runoff from higher reaches and will prove discouraging sites for garden beds without adequate drainage. On the other hand, ridges and hilltops tend to dry out quickly.

Climate

Regional climate dictates plant habitats. The roots of most temperate zone plants will grow as long as the temperature stays above 40° F. If it drops below that (or rises extremely high), plants stop growing. Temperature extremes can also retard the action of microorganisms that provide soil nutrients through the breakdown of organic material.

Rainfall variations also affect growth patterns, although moisture can be modified successfully by irrigation. The ideal garden soil allows most of the water to move through it and the excess to drain away; it's harder to establish such a relationship with clay or sandy soils.

The amount and intensity of sunlight and the rate of the air flow also create microenvironments within even a small space. Successful gardening calls for matching plants to these environments. For instance, if a plant description includes a phrase such as "needs some protection," you will want to know more.

If that extra protection is needed during the growing season, the plant should be placed in a location not exposed to prevailing winds or full sun during the hottest part of the day. If it needs extra protection during the winter, it may require mulch as well as shelter from harsh winds.

ANALYZING YOUR SOIL

One clue to the health of a potential garden site is the vegetation it supports. If there is a thick and healthy stand of weeds, both grassy and broad-leafed varieties, it should be an excellent location for growing edibles and ornamentals.

If vegetation is of only one species, or is sparse or lacking, the situation calls for some study. The problem could be environmental (too much shade or too little water) or soil-based (compacted, eroded, or toxic-poisoned ground, for instance).

After a superficial appraisal of conditions, take a good look at the soil. How deep is the topsoil? If it's thin, what does the soil underneath look like?

Pick up a handful of soil. Does it appear to hold sufficient moisture and air? Does it crumble easily? Would it be easy to till? If it falls apart after being squeezed, it can be spaded or tilled easily.

How about the texture? Would it be classified as clay, sand, or silt? Does it contain a good percentage of organic material, such as plant roots, manure, compost, leaves, stems, sawdust, or other substances? Any soil in its natural state contains some organic matter, but the proportions vary widely.

Sight and feel are two ways to analyze soil. Surprisingly, smell is also important. Take a whiff: Soils should smell sweet, not sour. They should smell like a warm spring day.

Soil Types

As mentioned previously, studying the soil helps gardeners determine what they have and what they need to do to improve it. A soil's properties depend upon its geological origin, age, the environment of the region, and its vegetative history—what plants have been growing there and for how long.

The character of the soil depends on the predominant size of the mineral particles and the amount of organic material it contains. The size, shape, and quantity of both the mineral and organic matter also helps determine the amounts of air and water in the soil.

As noted earlier, a soil's texture is classified by the size of its mineral particles, from clay to

Soil Texture Classifications

Percentages of sand, silt, and clay determine soil texture. Circles indicate approximate percentages of sand, silt, and clay in major soil texture classifications. The triangle can be used to classify specific soils.

Soil classifications do not change abruptly— one gradually eases into the next. For example, if your soil is about 15% clay, 65% sand, and 20% silt, it would be classified as "sandy loam" because the three percentage lines intersect at that point of the triangle.

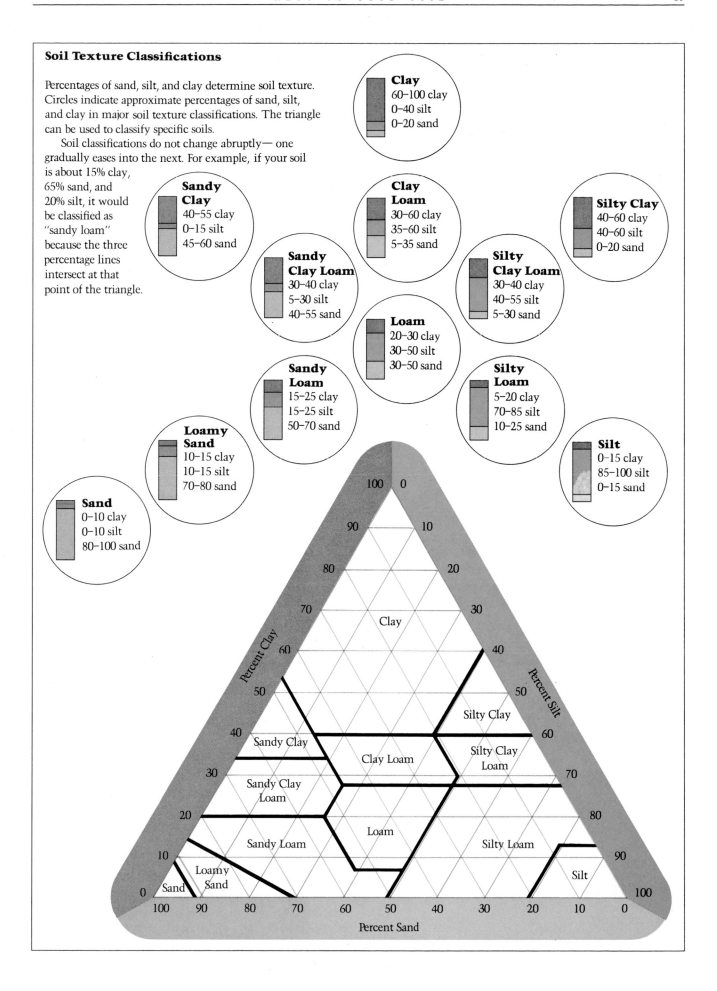

Clay
60–100 clay
0–40 silt
0–20 sand

Sandy Clay
40–55 clay
0–15 silt
45–60 sand

Clay Loam
30–60 clay
35–60 silt
5–35 sand

Silty Clay
40–60 clay
40–60 silt
0–20 sand

Sandy Clay Loam
30–40 clay
5–30 silt
40–55 sand

Silty Clay Loam
30–40 clay
40–55 silt
5–30 sand

Loam
20–30 clay
30–50 silt
30–50 sand

Sandy Loam
15–25 clay
15–25 silt
50–70 sand

Silty Loam
5–20 clay
70–85 silt
10–25 sand

Loamy Sand
10–15 clay
10–15 silt
70–80 sand

Silt
0–15 clay
85–100 silt
0–15 sand

Sand
0–10 clay
0–10 silt
80–100 sand

sand. It's rare that a soil is 100 percent sand, silt, or clay, so scientists have named the mixtures loamy sand, sandy loam, silty loam, loam, sandy clay loam, clay loam, silty clay loam, sandy clay, and silty clay.

Sandy loam, loam, and silty loam textures are the most desirable garden soils. They contain the right proportions for good water retention and percolation (drainage), aeration, and nutrient supply.

A simple experiment with fairly accurate results lets gardeners determine the texture of their soil (see the illustration below). Carry out this same test using soil from different places in your garden. Then chart each of the soil samples by marking off the layers on a piece of paper held up to the jar as shown and compare them to the soil texture triangle on page 19.

If the particles divide into about 40 percent sand, 40 percent silt, and 20 percent clay, the soil can be termed loam—the most desirable of all types. If it falls into another classification, it may require regular additions of organic matter to improve it (see page 28). Even loam needs organic matter from time to time.

Nutrient Levels

As mentioned earlier, plants need a number of nutrients, especially nitrogen, phosphorus, and potassium. They also require sufficient levels of calcium, magnesium, and a variety of micronutrients to grow normally.

The relative acidity or alkalinity of the soil has a great deal to do with how well nourished plants will be. That's why knowing the pH level (measure of acidity) of a soil is so important. Generally speaking, plants grow best in neutral to slightly acid garden soils, with a pH of 6.5 (slightly acid) to between 7.0 (neutral) and 7.2 (mildly alkaline).

There are two ways to determine the nutrient content and acid-alkaline quality of soil: Watch plants for a season to see if they achieve the desired growth, or have the soil tested—a much quicker and more reliable solution.

The only sure way to check the pH of a soil is by testing it. If it's tested by a professional laboratory (see below), the pH reading will be included in the report. Or you can check it yourself, using a commercial soil-testing kit or "electronic paper" (a significant advancement over litmus paper). Both are available in scientific supply stores and garden centers.

Soil Tests

A soil test offers valuable information to gardeners with soil-related problems in an established garden as well as to those who simply want to know what plants will grow most vigorously. A soil test is not a complicated process, and it's the only way to find out whether the soil has sufficient nutrients.

Testing laboratories   University agricultural extension services throughout the United States test soil samples for a nominal fee; for the address of your state office, see pages 108 and 109. In addition, some private soil-analysis laboratories offer testing for individuals, though their fees are usually higher. Look for them in the telephone directory under Laboratories–Testing.

The soil-testing office not only analyzes the soil, but also offers specific recommendations for improving it. The written analysis gives readings and interpretations for soil pH, organic content, and nitrogen, phosphorus, potassium, calcium, and magnesium levels. A sample test result is shown on pages 106 and 107.

When to test   For unimproved land, soil samples should be collected three to four months before planting. This allows ample time to get the report back from the laboratory and make any necessary soil improvements. In established gardens, this lead time is not necessary.

If basic fertility levels are maintained, soil tests need be made only every five years or so.

Determining Soil Texture

Fill a quart jar about ⅔ full of water. Add soil until the jar is almost full. Screw on the jar top and shake it vigorously. Then let the soil settle.

In twenty seconds the heaviest sand particles sink to the bottom and the sand layer becomes visible. The silt layer takes about two minutes to form, and the clay particles won't settle for several weeks. By measuring the settled-out layers at these times, gardeners can get a fairly accurate estimate of texture.

Note: It's important to start with dry soil and grind it as fine as possible. Adding a little water softener, which contains a dispersing agent, breaks up the chunks.

Taking a sample   Some extension offices and soil laboratories provide a written form, a special sample box, a soil probe, and a shipping carton along with instructions for taking and sending samples. If these are provided, follow the instructions faithfully; if not, collect soils as outlined below.

Let the ground dry out before collecting the samples. Otherwise, they will be too difficult to mix properly.

Use a clean spade and clean plastic pail; metal buckets might contain elements that would give misleading results. Push the spade deep into the soil. Throw aside the first spadeful of soil and with the spade cut a ½- to 1-inch slice from the back of the hole. The slice, which should be at least 7 inches deep and fairly even in width and thickness, goes into the pail.

Repeat this procedure five or six times in different places in the garden. Then thoroughly mix the slices in the pail. From this mixture, take about one pint of soil (you can use a sealable plastic bag) and let it dry. Mail or take the soil sample to the local extension office.

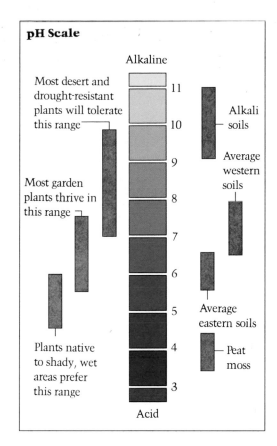

pH Scale

Alkaline

Most desert and drought-resistant plants will tolerate this range

Most garden plants thrive in this range

Plants native to shady, wet areas prefer this range

11
10
9
8
7
6
5
4
3

Acid

Alkali soils

Average western soils

Average eastern soils

Peat moss

Taking a Soil Sample

Use clean plastic pail and shovel to collect soil

Discard first spadeful. Then make ½″–1″ cut about 7″ deep.

Put soil in bucket and repeat process in other locations. Mix soil samples thoroughly.

Let soil dry completely. Put 1 pint mixed soil into plastic bag and seal top.

Fold and secure bag with rubber band

Mail or take sample to testing lab

Results should be returned in one to two weeks, depending on how busy the soil lab is. Results are likely to come back faster if soil samples are taken in October, November, or December, when there is far less rush than in the spring.

IDENTIFYING PROBLEM SOILS

Understanding soils helps gardeners achieve their ambitions. Although plants can be grown hydroponically (in water with nutrients), most plants grow in soil. Once gardeners learn how soil relates to plant growth, they can learn to "read" soils and discover what steps must be taken to improve their own garden.

Soils with a high percentage of clay or sand are well known for causing troubles for gardeners, but there are other offenders. The most common problem soils are described below. Solutions for correcting their deficiencies are offered in the chapter titled "Solving Soil Problems," starting on page 81.

Clay Soil

By picking up a wet handful of this "heavy" soil, it's easy to see how quickly it can be molded into shape. If squeezed, the slippery soil oozes through your fingers. Tilling is most easily accomplished when the soil is just moist; when dry, it's hard and crusty. But a clay soil does have advantages. It retains water and nutrients and its crumbly structure enables it to drain well. Unfortunately, it's often too compact with little room for water and air unless improved by regular additions of compost or other organic material. Clay soils are common in valleys and near watercourses.

Sandy Soil

Even when this gritty soil is damp, it barely holds together. Although a sandy soil is easy to cultivate, its large particles encourage water and air to pass through too swiftly, carrying away nutrients. Regular additions of compost or other organic matter slows up their rapid progress. Sandy soils are common in coastal states from Massachusetts south to Florida and along the Gulf of Mexico.

Acid Soil

If azaleas, blueberries, or other acid-loving plants are thriving, chances are the soil is acid, with a pH roughly between 5.0 and 6.0, well below the optimum 7.0 level. The relative acidity or alkalinity of soils is important, because it affects the availability of soluble salts supplying plant nutrients. If the pH is not correct for the plant, nutrients may be unavailable. Plants that can't tolerate acid soils appear stunted and have sparse roots. But sight and feel aren't enough to analyze this soil; it needs to be tested (see page 20). Acid soils are common in high-rainfall areas, such as the eastern and northwestern sections of the United States (see the map on page 103).

Alkaline Soil

Some plants grow well in a moderately alkaline soil with a pH level above the neutral point of 7.0, but if it's too alkaline, plants may become chlorotic (leaves develop yellow areas between their veins because the plants' roots are unable to take in the iron they need from the soil). Alkaline soils are most often found in areas receiving less than 20 inches of rain per year (see the map on page 103). The average pH of soils in the interior of the western United States is between 6.5 and slightly over 8.0. Soil testing (see page 20) is the best way to assess the pH level.

Although clay soil tends to compact unless amended, it retains moisture and offers a good environment for many plants, including these sedums and hens-and-chickens.

Top: Regular additions of organic matter help sandy soil retain moisture and nutrients.
Bottom: Azaleas and other acid-loving plants grow well in areas with heavy rainfall.

Alkali, or Sodic, Soil

Soils such as those found in the deserts of the Southwest are extremely alkaline, with a pH of 9.0 to 11.0. Their high concentration of free sodium destroys the soil structure and causes clay particles to lodge in soil pores, making the soil impermeable to water. A black crust may cover the soil surface. Gardening in this type of environment may be limited to raised beds or containers.

Saline Soil

A salty soil with too much sodium chloride (common table salt) or salts of calcium, magnesium, or potassium can burn plant foliage, stunt growth, and inhibit germination. Tissue at the edge of plant leaves turns yellow, then dies. These excess salts can come from natural soil minerals, irrigation water, fertilizers, or deicing compounds. When there is not enough rain, or if drainage is poor, they accumulate.

The thin soil of this hillside has been cleverly disguised by carefully positioned rocks edged with a colorful potpourri of ground covers.

Shallow Soil

A limited capacity to retain water causes shallow soil to dry quickly if on a slope, or drain poorly if on level ground. Shallow soils may be caused by underlying bedrock or a hard, impervious layer of soil called hardpan (see next column). Although small and shallow-rooted plants can be grown successfully in shallow soil, larger plants need more depth. Large trees, for example, require 1½ to 4 feet or more of soil to anchor roots securely.

Eroded Soil

Water and wind can erode bare soil. The steeper the slope, the more severe its erosion by water; the drier it is, the easier it is for the wind to carry it off.

Rocky Soil

A rocky terrain usually doesn't affect plant growth, although it can make the ground difficult to till and plant. The only noncompatible planting would be a root crop, such as beets or carrots, which requires soil with a consistent texture to keep from becoming deformed.

Compacted Soil

Topsoil becomes compacted by the movement of heavy equipment and by constant foot traffic. When a soil is packed down, it loses its porous structure, inhibiting the circulation of air and water. Roots grow poorly, if at all, in compacted soil.

Hardpan

This soil is well named. Hard and only a few inches to no more than 1 foot thick, it's basically impenetrable to both plant roots and water. Even if the soil's surface is fairly permeable, a layer of hardpan beneath would inhibit proper drainage. Trees and large plants growing over hardpan have shallow roots and are easily blown over in high winds. Poor cultivation methods can cause hardpan.

Nutrient Deficiencies

As mentioned before, soils lacking in nutrients do not support healthy plant growth. Although symptoms vary, if plant growth is less than ideal, nutrient deficiencies might be suspected. A soil test is the way to check this problem.

A brilliant perennial, Penstemon rupicola (beardtongue), grows well in shallow, well-drained soil.

Grand-Scale Success Stories

Public gardens may look eternal, but they didn't always exist and are rarely located on ideal growing sites. The stories of the creation of several of the country's most beautiful gardens should inspire all gardeners. They are classic examples of the importance of improving garden soils.

Brooklyn Botanic Garden

Case in point is this 50-acre urban oasis located in the heart of New York City. One of the world's great botanic gardens, the park, founded in 1910, serves as Brooklyn's largest cultural attraction. Hundred of thousands of visitors arrive annually to see its vast collections.

Who would possibly guess that it was constructed on land with extremely poor soil? The cost of hauling in topsoil would have been not only prohibitively expensive, but also not particularly scientific. Therefore, the advice of an expert from the Federal Bureau of Soils was sought. His recommendations stressed adding both fertilizers and organic matter.

During the first year, weeds and grass were allowed to grow until July or August, with gardeners mowing often enough to prevent seed formation. They left the mown grass and weeds on the ground, then plowed and harrowed them into the ground along with lime and large quantities of manure. A few weeks later, they disked and harrowed again.

In early autumn, they sowed ryegrass and, in early spring of the second year, plowed the rye under when it was 8 to 10 inches high. It soon began to decompose.

Gardeners next applied ground phosphate, harrowing it deeply into the soil. Then fertilizer—a mixture of dried blood, acid phosphate, high-grade tankage, and potash—was spread at the rate of 500 pounds per acre. Once the fertilizer was harrowed into the soil, a heavy stand of bluegrass and white clover was planted, allowed to grow through the winter, and then plowed and disked under a final time.

The following spring, the now-fertile soil, rebuilt through a combination of cover cropping, fertilizing, and cultivating, was ready for planting. The cost of following the soil expert's recommendations proved to be only a fraction of what topsoil would have cost.

Chicago Botanic Garden

When an agreement was made in 1965 to turn Cook County Forest Preserve land into a botanic garden, a different sort of soil problem was presented. Poor drainage was, and is, the primary soil problem, since the property was marshy lowland. It was described by forest preserve conservationists as "alternately flooded, mosquito-ridden, and finally drained. Periodic bog fires burned endlessly, constituting a well-remembered nuisance for area residents."

During the next three years, heavy equipment moved earth and diverted water to create a new landscape of hills, islands, and lakes from depleted fields and polluted waterways. The task was formidable. The extensive working of the soggy land with heavy equipment compacted the clay soils, destroyed soil structure, and made the drainage worse.

Dealing with the poor drainage is an ongoing challenge handled project by project, garden by garden, and plant by plant. Each time a tree, shrub, or garden bed is installed, the staff must build a separate drainage system.

Drainage tiles, consisting of plastic tubing dotted with holes, are wrapped in landscape fabric to keep the holes from clogging. Set in beds of gravel, the drainage tiles run the entire lengths of garden beds and from the bases of trees and shrubs out to the many lagoons.

In perimeter areas, soil preparation is minimal other than breaking up existing soil for planting trees and shrubs; in new garden beds, man-made soils are added. The process begins by digging and removing the top 18 inches of the soil. Then a drainage system is installed. The soil is replaced with a combination of 35 to 50 percent topsoil, compost, peat moss, pine bark, and calcite clay (pelletized kitty litter). Calcite clay works better than sand to improve clay soil.

A commonly used formula is 50 percent soil, 30 percent compost, and 20 percent calcite clay. For mulch, gardeners use leaves and, increasingly, landscape waste bought from area villages. The mulch is prepared in a tub grinder and applied directly to beds and borders.

The garden tests its soils on a regular basis and usually does not fertilize until after assessing test results.

Golden Gate Park

The soil success story of Golden Gate Park in San Francisco is another case of building landscaped gardens on a very inhospitable site. Three miles long and a half-mile wide and consisting of arid sand dunes with little vegetation, the park was considered a poor deal when acquired by the city in 1868. But there were pluses: It sloped toward the ocean, assuring good drainage; fresh water was abundant; and the prevailing western wind provided good air circulation.

In the park's earliest days, winds combined with drifting sands made the land hard to cultivate and harder still to enjoy. Aside from a few hundred trees, mostly willows, and some grasses and shrubs, its western end was bare of vegetation. On the hilly east side, oak, wild cherry, lupines, and wild strawberries grew in a thin layer of topsoil. Erosion and lack of organic material were major problems.

In 1870, William Hammond Hall, the first superintendent of parks, created a naturalistic design patterned closely after New York's Central Park. For the next six years, he rebuilt the soil using horse manure from city streets. At the same time, he began planting grasses and shrubs to stabilize the soil and serve as windbreaks.

Victim of political intrigue, Hall was forced to resign in 1876 but came back in power in 1886 and appointed John McLaren, a young Scotsman, his successor. McLaren was to spend 56 years of his 97-year life continuing Hall's work.

An experienced landscape designer and grower, McLaren learned to tie down the sand with seabent grass from Europe. He then applied layers of topsoil to hold bluegrass and cypress and other native trees. At the same time, he continued to build the soil through the addition of horse manure and other organic materials. By lining sandy excavations with many loads of clay, he created the Chain of Lakes area.

Stopping the wind erosion of the sandy dunes and building the soil were the two big challenges in creating this park. Creating windbreaks by molding the landscape and then planting grasses, shrubs, and trees was an ongoing challenge.

Three of the country's premier gardens overcame major soil problems. Top left: It took Brooklyn Botanic Garden more than a year to build topsoil. Top right: Drainage is an ongoing challenge at Chicago Botanic Garden. Bottom: Thin topsoil, erosion, and a lack of organic matter were major concerns at San Francisco's Golden Gate Park.

Raised beds offer many advantages, including better drainage, warmer soil temperature, easier cultivation, and plant protection.

HANDLING DRAINAGE PROBLEMS

Poor drainage is easy to diagnose: Water stands in puddles or is sluggish in soaking into the ground. These soggy soils deserve extra attention, since they can defeat otherwise stalwart gardeners.

Plants that require good drainage will dwindle, wilt, and die when grown in perpetually wet soils. Their root systems need air as well as water to perform their vital functions. When the water takes up the greatest volume of soil pore space, it leaves insufficient room for air, and the plants literally drown.

Clay, alkaline, and other soils that develop a crust on their surface when dry usually drain poorly. Compacted, shallow, hardpan, and layered soils (those composed of radically differing textures) also have drainage problems. Finally, poor drainage often occurs around natural springs or in areas with high water tables.

Testing Drainage

If poor drainage is suspected, the soil should be tested. Dig a hole 1 to 2 feet deep, fill it with water, and watch how quickly it drains into the soil. If the water doesn't drain at the rate of 1 inch or more an hour, the drainage is considered poor, and the reason will have to be found and corrected.

There are two ways to correct drainage problems: by amending the soil or physically reshaping the ground.

Soil-Amending Solutions

Drainage problems due to heavy soils high in clay particles can be greatly improved by amendments of organic matter, such as manure, compost, peat moss, or nitrogen-stabilized sawdust (extra nitrogen added to make up for what is lost in the process of decomposition). A combination of organic amendments and mulching will also solve the problem for soils that crust on the surface.

Two to four inches of organic matter worked into the heavy soil each year opens it up and improves its structure, allowing better drainage. The chapter titled "Preparing the Soil," starting on page 33, gives complete details on all types of organic soil amendments.

Similarly, many compacted soils can be improved with regular amendments of organic matter. This soil should be tilled to loosen it before the organic matter is added. If compaction was

All eyes are directed to the ornamentals in this attractive berm. The aboveground environment simplifies both watering and weeding.

caused by heavy construction equipment, the soil may have to be tilled as deep as 2 feet or more, a job best done by a professional landscape contractor.

Hardpan also calls for physical solutions before the soil can be amended. Sometimes, it can be broken up by having holes drilled through it with a soil auger. If the layer is too thick, you may need to call in a professional to help design a drainage system on top of the hardpan.

The problem of poor drainage in shallow soils in low-lying areas can be solved in a number of ways, including a regular program of heavy organic amendments to build up the soil to a depth that will support all of the desired plantings.

Another solution—and one that would also work for hardpan, compacted, and shallow soils—is to create raised beds or berms atop the compacted areas. This method, described on page 31, is often easier and less expensive than amending the soil.

Alkali soils (those with high concentrations of free sodium, which destroys soil structure) can be improved by cultivating gypsum into the soil at the rate of 5 pounds for every 100 square feet. Cultivate well and then water thoroughly to leach out the sodium. Repeat the procedure until the drainage is improved significantly. Then add organic amendments.

Testing Drainage

Dig a hole 1′–2′ deep, fill with water, and see how quickly it drains. One inch per hour is satisfactory.

*One solution to soggy
soil problems is to
create a water garden
starring plants
that grow well with
wet feet.*

Physical Solutions

Raised beds, terraces, retaining walls, earth shaping, drainage-tile systems, and garden pools all offer imaginative solutions to poorly draining soils. Because these are both design and construction projects, it often pays to have them done by professional garden landscaping companies.

Raised beds   One ideal way to cope with soil problems is to build a plant bed above the ground level, even atop pavement, decks, or roofs. Raised beds allow you to control soil depth, texture, and structure while assuring that the nutrient and water needs of plants are being met. Prepare the beds from mounded heaps of topsoil or commercial soil mixes and confine them by constructed forms of wood, brick, or cinder block.

Berms   Like raised beds, berms create a new, hospitable root environment atop problem soils. This unconfined, mounded earth bed also serves as a major design feature in any landscape plan, so it's important to plan its construction carefully. Berms often serve as sight barriers.

Terraces   Retaining walls and terraces are a successful solution to problem soil on sloping or eroded ground. Keep the topography of the land in mind when planning this project.

Water gardens   Low-lying, poorly draining areas make logical sites for garden pools or bog gardens. This increasingly popular garden element needs careful planning to be successful. Even though flexible plastic liner has made pool construction easier, preparing the excavation and installing the liner and coping (top edging) usually calls for the assistance of a professional contractor.

Drainage-tile systems   Drainage tiles, such as those used by the Chicago Botanic Garden (see page 26), may be the solution for soggy soils in areas with high water tables. These underground systems are also good ways to correct specific problems during heavy rains, such as dripping roofs and overloaded downspouts. The key is to plan the trenches so that the water is directed toward lower runoff sites where it can do no harm.

Light, airy astilbe is often planted poolside. This perennial grows in sun or shade and needs cool, moist soil.

Moisture-Loving Plants

Plants that prefer moist soils are ideal choices for sites ranging from often damp to usually wet. Oddly, many plants that do well in soggy soils are also adaptable to a wide variety of other garden conditions. Impatiens cultivars, for example, are excellent annual choices for wet soils in shady to partially shady sites. The list below indicates some good choices for wet soils in certain climate zones (see map on page 103). If water or bog gardens are chosen as physical solutions for the problem area, another palette of plants could be added, including waterlilies, lotuses, cattails, arrowheads, and horsetails.

Trees		Zones
Betula nigra	River birch	4–9
Liquidamber styraciflua	American sweet gum	5–9
Quercus bicolor	Swamp white oak	3–8
Quercus palustris	Pin oak	4–8
Salix alba	White willow	2–8
Salix babylonica	Weeping willow	6–8
Taxodium distichum	Bald cypress	4–8
Shrubs		
Clethra alnifolia	Summersweet	3–9
Cornus alba 'Siberica'	Siberian dogwood	2–8
Ilex verticillata 'Winter Red'	Winterberry	4–8
Tamerix ramosissima	Tamarisk	2–6
Perennials		
Aruncus dioicus	Goatsbeard	4
Astilbe × *arendsii*	Astilbe	5
Carex	Sedges	6, 7
Filipendula ulmaria	Queen-of-the-meadow	3
Iris	Iris, crested, Japanese	4, 5
Ligularia dentata	Bigleaf goldenray	4
Miscanthus sinensis	Maidenhairgrasses	5
Spartina pectinata	Prairie cordgrass	5
Osmunda regalis	Royal fern	3–10
Annuals		
Ionopsidium acaule	Diamond flower	
Nemophilia merziesii	Baby-blue-eyes	

Preparing the Soil

Tilling, composting, mulching—the fundamentals of improving garden soils are essentially the same for all gardens. Organic soil amendments improve the texture and drainage of soils ranging from clay to sand.

An orderly sequence of building and improving soil makes it easier to plant and maintain a healthy garden. The single most important method of soil improvement is the incorporation of organic matter into the soil as an amendment or conditioner and as a mulch spread over the soil surface. Beneficial soil microorganisms break down this organic matter, binding together the soil particles in the process.

To a gardener, organic matter refers to any material derived from living organisms. The term usually includes manures, leaves, grasses, commercial plant residue, and other plant debris. Organic compost and sphagnum peat moss are among the best organic soil conditioners. This chapter also looks at other amendments that can play important roles in building an ideal soil, including those that correct an acid or alkaline soil by altering its pH level.

The addition of organic matter tilled into the soil to a depth of 6 inches improves the texture and structure of all types of soil, from sand to clay. Although many organic materials fulfill the twin roles of soil amending and fertilizing, it should be pointed out that fertilizers (discussed in the next chapter) and soil amendments are not one and the same. Amendments improve a soil's ability to supply nutrients and water to plants. Manufactured fertilizers provide the nutrients, but don't improve soil structure.

Adding amendments is one of the most reliable methods for improving problem soil and providing a hospitable underground environment for plants.

Good drainage and improved soil structure, texture, and fertility are the goals of soil preparation. The following pages offer advice and recommendations for preparing a good garden base, from tilling the soil through composting and mulching. The chapter also describes methods of making potting mix for container plants and garden beds and shows the proper tools for use with every job.

A well-chosen mulch protects plants, reduces weed growth, and grooms the garden, but soils can be overmulched, which leads to pests and diseases. Included here are tips on when and how to mulch to the best advantage.

WORKING THE SOIL

If plant root systems are to perform their vital roles, providing physical support and taking in nutrients, moisture, and air, the soil must be hospitable to those roots. It should be friable, quick to crumble, and have good tilth—a structure and texture that make it easy to cultivate.

Tilling generally refers to the deeper plowing and turning of soil, a process necessary for improving texture and working in amendments. Cultivating—a term that refers to the whole process of preparing soils for crops—is often used more selectively to describe the hoeing or shallow turning of the soil surface to

A spade for turning and moving soil and a fork for loosening soil and rotating compost are two essential cultivating tools.

keep weeds from competing with desirable plants. Proper tilling incorporates amendments into the soil, improves structure, and also gets rid of weeds.

Tools of the Trade

Because of the wide variety of mechanized and hand tools on the market for tilling and cultivating the soil, gardeners will want to take time to study and test them. If possible, it's a good idea to try out tools in a garden situation.

The size and needs of the projects plus time and budget constraints dictate gardeners' choices. Experienced gardeners know that it pays to buy the best quality tools available. These sturdier (and probably more expensive) tools will last much longer than less expensive models.

Cleanliness is next to godliness where garden tools are concerned. Always keep them clean, sharp, and in good repair. A thin coat of lightweight oil or kerosene keeps blades from rusting. If you often forget to bring tools inside, add a touch of bright paint to their handles so that they can be spotted quickly. Power equipment should also be well maintained. For fast service of power tools, take them into the repair shop in the off-season.

Hand tools for tilling include shovels, spades, forks, and trowels. Most people use the words *spade* and *shovel* interchangeably, but there is a difference.

Spade   This handy tool comes in many styles. Spades have almost flat, rectangular blades, usually a D-grip handle, and often a shorter handle than shovels. They are handy for digging, turning, cutting, and lifting soil. The rectangular blade also makes them useful for edging beds and deep cultivating. In fact, many gardeners consider spades more useful in garden work than shovels. Serious gardeners usually have a selection of both.

Shovel   One of the gardener's most useful tools, shovels come in a great variety of styles and shapes. They have curved blades that may be blunt, pointed, or rounded, and handles with plain or D-grips. Because of the concave blade, shovels are the tools of choice when moving soils and other loose materials from one place to another. They are also handy for digging beds, planting, and working with compost.

Tool Collection

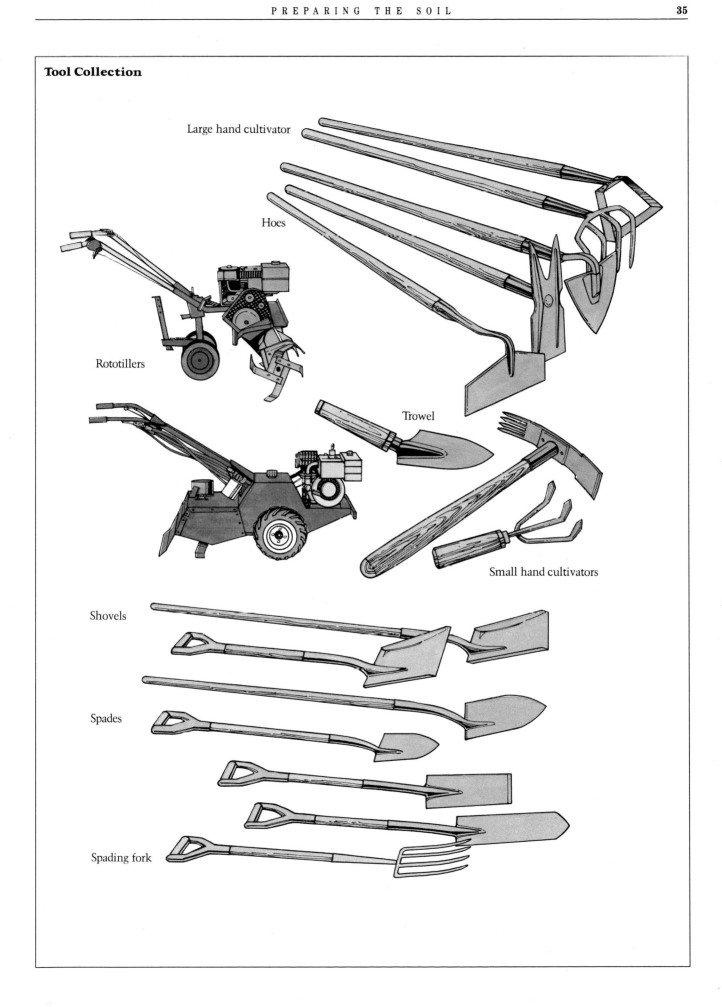

Large hand cultivator

Hoes

Rototillers

Trowel

Small hand cultivators

Shovels

Spades

Spading fork

Spading fork Garden and spading forks have D-grip handles and four flat, long tines in a wide head. They're particularly helpful when turning over garden soil, breaking up heavy soil, and digging out plants with roots intact.

Trowel These small, short-handled garden tools with metal scoops at the working end look like miniature shovels. Trowels are ideal for tilling and cultivating small areas, container gardens, and raised beds. Once the soil has been prepared, a gardener may need no more than a trowel to plant seeds and seedlings and to add and work fertilizers into the soil.

Hand cultivators These tools, used primarily during the growing season for weeding, include hoes, pronged cultivators, long-handled cultivators, push-pull weeder-cultivators, and wheeled cultivators.

Mechanized tools Rotary tillers include an array of front-wheeled and rear-wheeled gas-engine machines, many of which are available for sale or rent. It's wise to try them out before buying, since these tillers represent a far greater investment than do hand tools.

If garden beds are large and time is a factor, investing in power tools for other types of garden cultivation might make sense. Anyone considering such a purchase should check various consumer publications and visit major garden centers to see what's available.

Tilling Methods

In most cases, tilling the soil to prepare it for seeding and planting involves applying and mixing in several inches of organic amendments, fertilizers, and any materials needed to correct pH. This can be done simply by digging, turning, and mixing with hand tools. But when working with shallow topsoil or where there is a marked difference between topsoil and subsoil, soil amendments should be mixed not only into surface soil but also subsoil.

Double-digging An old English method called double-digging mixes topsoil and subsoil to the depth of double the spade blade. It's hard work and most gardeners limit it to a few beds at a time. But double-digging (illustrated on page 93) is the best way to handcultivate a new garden with poor soil.

Using a wheelbarrow Another popular method for tilling soil for raised beds or container gardening is to use a wheelbarrow or other container as a mixing bowl, and simply stir together the planting medium of choice. Planting soils might range from three parts topsoil and one part peat moss or compost to a totally nonsoil mix of two parts peat moss, one part sand, and one part perlite.

Controlling Weeds

When cultivating vegetable or ornamental beds to control weeds, a number of methods are possible. Chances are you'll use all of them. Weeds can be grubbed out by hand, an easy task if the soil is friable and moist, or cut with a small knife or special weeding tool. They can also be tilled or scuffled out with hoes.

Weeding chores are simplified by the regular use of mulches, which control weeds by covering the seeds too deeply to allow germination (see the illustration on page 47). But if weeds are persistent throughout the garden, it might be a good idea to use an herbicide, such as glyphosate (known by the trade names of Kleenup® or Roundup®).

Applied to actively growing weed foliage during warm weather, glyphosate kills the plant within two to four days. Treated areas can be tilled and planted in a week. One precaution: Glyphosate kills any plant it touches. Don't use it indiscriminately; read the label closely and follow directions precisely.

Tilling Cautions

Overtilling or cultivating at the wrong time can destroy garden soil. Mechanized rotary tillers, though invaluable for cultivating soil when used properly, can damage its structure if overused. They pulverize soil to such a degree that it loses the porous quality needed for water and air circulation. Pulverized soils are easily compacted when wet.

Rotary tillers can also create hardpan below their blades, spoiling soil drainage. In addition, tilling can expose weed seeds.

When using these excellent labor-saving devices, remember not to overtill and to cultivate the soil when it's moist and clumpy, neither too wet nor too dry. In fact, it's not advisable to cultivate wet soils with any tools. Soils heavy with high proportions of clay are particularly susceptible to structural damage if tilled when wet. It's all too easy to destroy the peds, those crumbly aggregates so vital to soil structure. Once this structure is destroyed, the soil compacts easily.

Garden soils should have good tilth; that is, they should be easy to cultivate and have a moist, crumbly texture. Wet soils are fragile. Even a small trowel can destroy their air spaces, compact them, and ruin their drainage.

When working in the garden, remember that heavy foot traffic compacts soils, especially clay soils with a fine texture. Any garden plan incorporating large beds should include walkways. Such handy paths can be attractive additions to the garden when designed with materials such as stepping-stones. But even planks laid atop the ground when working the soil minimize compaction by spreading weight over a large area.

SOIL AMENDMENTS

Amendments are substances worked into the soil in order to encourage plant growth by improving soil structure and texture. Soils benefit most from the addition of organic matter, such as compost, leaf mold, sawdust, manure, and sewage sludge. As a side benefit, these amendments may contain plant nutrients; in most cases, however, they are added to improve the physical characteristics of the soil. Although some soils are naturally better than others, all benefit from regular additions of organic matter.

Organic gardening is not new. Before chemists learned to make fertilizers and soil scientists discovered chemical means of making soils more hospitable to plant growth, farmers and home gardeners were working animal manures and cover crops into their soils.

Unless a garden site has been well maintained over a number of years, soil amendments will be necessary for growing most vegetables, fruits, and ornamental plants. (Although fertilizers supply plant nutrients, they do not improve the physical qualities of soil.) In all gardens, in order to maintain a high quality of plant growth, the soil should be amended regularly with organic matter to maintain and further improve its texture and structure.

Inorganic Amendments

To improve garden soil and keep it in good condition, inorganic amendments may also be required. Lime, a substance containing calcium

and oxygen, is used to sweeten sour soils. That's another way of saying that it raises the pH by increasing the alkalinity of soils that are too acid. Conversely, sulfur in a variety of forms lowers soil pH, increasing acidity in alkaline soils.

Gypsum, a soft, soluble compound of calcium, is a valuable amendment for improving sodic, saline, and certain clay soils. When added with organic matter, gypsum improves the structure and drainage of sodic soils and also may help the drainage of heavy clay soils.

Fertilizers as Amendments

Although not thought of as soil amendments, fertilizers (described in detail in the next chapter) should be considered whenever soil improvement is contemplated. Fertilizers may be either organic or inorganic. Plants respond equally to nutrients, whether they come from chemical fertilizers or organic matter.

Gardeners may need to work ground limestone into the soil to correct the pH balance.

A rich-looking top-dressing, sphagnum peat moss is one of the most commonly applied soil conditioners.

The growing of vegetables and fruits removes many valuable nutrients from the soil each year. If these plants are to continue producing well, the nutrients must be replaced. Ornamentals fare better, although they too suffer a loss.

Value of Organic Matter

The benefits of adding organic matter to the soil are myriad. Organic matter is considered by many horticultural experts as the soil's unifying element. In unfertilized soils, organic matter is the major source of nitrogen and can be a big supplier of phosphorus and sulfur.

Organic matter is the glue that binds soil aggregates together, producing the granular structure that permits good circulation of water and air and allows roots to grow without obstruction. It also attracts and holds nutrients and trace elements, reducing losses due to leaching.

Organic matter increases a soil's capacity for retaining moisture. It also helps to make micronutrients available to plants. Some parts of organic matter are even transformed into substances that stimulate plant growth.

In the form of soil humus, organic matter acts as a buffer against sudden changes in acidity, alkalinity, salinity, temperature, and moisture. It also buffers damage due to pesticides or heavy metals.

When used as a mulch on top of soils, organic matter reduces moisture loss and erosion and moderates soil temperature, keeping the ground warmer in winter and cooler in summer. In arctic climes, soils need a thick top layer of organic matter to remain stable. If that covering is removed or destroyed, soils become warmer and permafrost melts, causing surface and pothole erosion.

Healthy soils with a good percentage of organic matter have multitudes of microscopic organisms, most of them beneficial. Some 4,000 different species have been identified. Organic matter stimulates their growth and supplies carbon, which enables them to perform their valuable functions.

Some of these organisms convert nitrogen from the air into water-soluble compounds that can be used by plants; some live symbiotically with plant roots, helping them find mineral nutrients; others produce substances useful to plants as a result of their own metabolism. Some microscopic organisms prey on harmful plant pathogens; still more are vital to soil aggregation by binding together organic matter and mineral particles.

Organic Matter Drawbacks

Although the benefits of using organic matter clearly outweigh the drawbacks, organic matter is not always beneficial to plant growth. It can serve as food for disease-bearing organisms living in the soil. Also, some plants are allelopathic (produce poisons, called phytotoxins, which damage other plants) and should not be used to amend soils.

One of the best-known examples of these phytotoxins is juglone, produced by the black walnut. The benefit to the plant is clear; juglone eliminates plant competition around the tree. Some common weeds also have allelopathic effects on garden plants. Giant foxtailgrass and common nutsedge inhibit the development of corn, and leafy spurge deters tomato growth.

COMPOST

The simplest, most inexpensive way to improve soils is to make a compost from leaves, grass clippings, plant prunings, weeds, and other plant debris. Of all the cultivation processes, composting is the most important. It requires little space, and there are many easy methods to convert garden waste material into fragrant, crumbly, nutrient-rich, and partially decomposed organic material.

Essentially, composting is a method of hurrying the natural decay of organic material by aerobic (oxygen-using) bacteria, and employing the end product, humus, to supplement the soil's organic content and improve its structure and texture. It's also a good way of utilizing material that otherwise would be classed as trash. Where local ordinances ban grass clippings and other plant debris from trash-collection sites, composting is the answer.

Compost can be applied to soil without fear of overfertilizing. An annual application rate of 250 to 500 pounds for each 1,000 square feet would not be too much. Unlike some chemical fertilizers, too-generous applications of compost won't burn plant foliage or roots.

What to Use

All plant matter eventually decomposes, but when making compost it's best to choose and prepare materials that speed up the process as fast as possible. Although composting requires moisture for plant materials to decompose, the composted material should not be too damp or anaerobic bacteria will multiply, producing a rank, rotting odor.

Leaves, grass clippings, and soft plant stalks and stems are valuable compost additions, but they need some preparation. Clippings should be fairly dry and mixed with other material to avoid odor and fly problems. Soft leaves should be shredded in advance to keep them from matting into tough, thick layers.

Soft, succulent plant material produces finished compost far faster than woody plants or chips, which decompose very slowly. Chipping or shredding makes the latter easier to handle.

What Not to Use

Seek a balance in the materials you compost, avoiding those that will not decompose rapidly, such as large pieces of wood, brush, and other debris. If large amounts of high-acid plant material, such as oak leaves or pine needles, are used, they should be shredded and lime should be added to neutralize the compost pile.

Don't include any toxic materials, such as plant material treated with persistent pesticides. Diseased plants should not be composted, since some organisms are resistant to the temperatures generated in most hot piles. In cold-weather areas where roads are salted, avoid including materials that might have been affected. Vegetable waste from the kitchen makes good compost, but don't use animal waste, since its smell attracts scavengers.

Top: Wood chips can be used as mulch and a soil conditioner. Bottom: These strawberry plants are mulched with ground wood bark.

Hot Composting

This method of composting produces the greatest amount of rich organic matter in the shortest period of time. In this process, plant debris is piled into a heap and managed so that the decomposition generates enough heat (140° F) to encourage the speedy transformation of organic matter into humus. The heat produced also kills weed seeds and disease-causing organisms.

The pile must be large enough to maintain the inside heat it produces. A 3-foot cube is about the smallest mass you can use to generate the proper temperature. A pile measuring 4 to 5 feet on the bottom and rising up to 4 feet is even better.

When building a compost heap, each layer of plant matter should be topped with a thin layer of high-quality garden soil for best results. This improves the texture of the compost and assures getting the proper number of microorganisms that do the actual work of decomposition.

The compost pile should be turned thoroughly at least once a month with a large garden fork to aerate the mixture and push outside matter into the center. Turning a compost heap is hard work but it's essential for hot composting. The compost must have enough air or the process of decay comes to a halt.

Spring through autumn are prime seasons for hot composting. It's impossible to keep the compost working in very cold weather.

A simple recipe for compost is one part shredded, dried plant material (leaves, twigs, and fine woody matter) and one part green plant matter (grass clippings, weeds, and trimmings) plus water and air. This combination contains about the right ratio of carbon and nitrogen needed to heat the pile and ensure its decomposition.

Lack of nitrogen is the most common cause of failed hot composting. Adding manure to the mix is one way to get extra nitrogen. Blood meal and cottonseed meal are other alternatives. Grass clippings are high in nitrogen; leaves are comparatively low.

Other common causes for compost failure are the size of the pile (insufficient mass for creating and retaining heat), type of material (too tough to decompose readily), or too little or too much moisture.

Experts recommend that compost have the consistency of a damp sponge. Too little moisture and the plant matter will not decompose; too much and there's too little air. If the top of a compost heap is slightly concave, it collects the most moisture. Rain and supplemental water will gather in the depression and seep slowly through the pile.

The rate of organic decomposition varies depending on the materials, air supply, temperature, and moisture. New material can be worked into the pile as it is aerated each month. Aged manure or a nitrogen-rich fertilizer can be added to each 6-inch-deep layer when the pile is turned. As the compost is formed, it will remain on the bottom of the pile as "soil" if you're using a pitchfork, or it can be worked back into the pile as a source of microorganisms required for decomposition.

Cold Composting

This method of decomposing plant material—more haphazard than hot composting—is easier and conserves nitrogen and humus, but it takes longer. Cold composting means quite simply piling up leaves and other organic material and forgetting them. By adding a layer of soil between layers of this organic matter, you keep the pile loose enough for adequate air circulation and ensure that the necessary bacteria and fungi are on hand. Because the biological action is lower with this method, it may take as long as a year or so before the organic matter can be applied to the soil.

If space allows, gardeners can prepare cold compost by digging a trench, filling it with plant residue and covering it with soil. One year later you can plant directly into this rich humus, or it can be removed and used elsewhere. Variations on this theme could be the smart gardener's way of preparing a new garden bed.

Compost Bin

A simple recipe for compost combines one part green matter with one part shredded, dried matter. Top each layer with a high-quality soil to assure decomposition.

Sheet Composting

Though slower than hot composting, sheet composting is useful for preparing sizable uncultivated areas. Layers of organic matter are spread on top of the soil and then tilled in to a depth of 1 foot or so. The organic matter decomposes slowly in the soil rather than in a compost heap.

To prepare, cut down any weeds or plants growing on the plot. Then layer 4 to 5 inches of leaves, grass, or other plant debris (shredded if necessary) on top of the soil. Add any other soil amendments and fertilizers, such as manure, before the material is turned into the soil, either by hand or with a mechanized tiller. The process of decomposition may deplete some soil nitrogen, so a nitrogen-rich fertilizer, such as blood meal or cottonseed meal, is a good soil supplement.

Green Manure

This process is similar to sheet composting, but it involves growing a winter cover crop that can be tilled into the soil in time for it to decompose before spring planting. Good choices for cover crops include legumes (high in nitrogen),

Mulching around ornamentals helps retain moisture and retard weed growth.

This generous compost bin has separate compartments for incoming organic material, working compost, and the finished product.

Green Manure

Cover crop is tilled into soil to return nutrients and organic matter

clovers, winter peas, cowpeas, lespedeza, and vetch. Buckwheat, rye and oat grains, and annual grasses such as rye and sudan are additional options.

Cover crops have other advantages. They halt erosion of bare ground, diminish the leaching of nutrients by autumn rains, and discourage weed growth. These crops should be planted after the regular growing season, in late summer or early autumn.

Cover crops and sheet compost should be tilled into the soil at least six weeks before planting a garden. It's even better to plant cover crops or turn sheet compost into the soil the summer before planting. It should be noted that no matter how good these compost methods are, the rate of soil improvement depends on the soil's original condition.

Commercial Organic Compost

Garden centers sell several commercial organic products to improve soil structure and texture and add nutrients. These are valuable products for gardeners who don't want to make their own compost or who want to begin gardening before their compost has finished working. Among the choices are dried manure and sphagnum peat moss.

Because peat moss and dried manure are both extremely dry, water must be added before the amendments are tilled into the soil. Open the bags and add water equal to about one half to one third the size of the bag. (Sphagnum peat moss can absorb twenty times its weight in water.) Let the bag stand for a few hours and then check. The peat moss or manure should be moist but not wet. Work it into the soil to a depth of 6 to 8 inches.

Other dried, ground, or shredded commercial composts may be produced locally from organic waste products. Check your area to see what's available. Because it's difficult to tell exactly what's in a product or how well it will meet the needs of a specific soil, it's a good idea to test it in a small area of the garden before distributing it widely.

Many companies recommend adding bioactivators to compost heaps. These harmless products are particularly helpful when good garden soils are lacking. They provide nitrogen, protein, and microorganisms that do the work of decomposition. Fertile garden soil and compost both contain multitudes of these microorganisms and enzymes, so a thin layer of soil or compost is equally as effective as an activator. Other natural sources of nitrogen and protein are bone and blood meals, alfalfa meal, and cottonseed meal.

Compost Bins and Composters

Some gardeners build pits or bins for their compost piles. Others use commercial bins. The three-sectioned bin shown on page 40 holds new, working, and finished material. Where space is at a premium, a compost bin with a tightfitting lid could also serve as an oversized garden bench.

Manufacturers of the classic manufactured composter, a ventilated drum that can be turned easily, claim that it creates compost from plant debris in a matter of only three to four weeks. That timing, as with any regular hot composting, depends on temperature and moisture conditions.

Easy-to-use wire and wooden bins fill the bill for people with room for an outdoor utility area. To cook the compost faster, place it into a reusable black plastic liner with perforated sides and an open bottom. These liners are specially manufactured to fit the bin.

Piles of rich organic matter are ready to be worked into the soil of this contoured garden.

Small-space dwellers use such creative composters as plastic bags and trash containers to work small amounts of green plant material. Trash bags can even be used to create compost anaerobically (in an airless environment). If you choose this alternative, be sure that the bag contains one-half brown material (shredded twigs, dried leaves, and so forth) as well as green leaves, vegetative garbage, and other plant debris. Close the bag tightly, place it in a sunny spot, and rotate it every day. This process can be smelly if interrupted before decomposition is completed.

CORRECTING pH

As a general rule, the eastern and northwestern parts of the country have soils that are more acid, or sour, than those of the southwestern and interior parts of the country, which are inclined toward alkaline, or sweet, soils. But a soil test is the only sure way to discover the pH of a garden.

Overly acidic or alkaline soils inhibit the plant's ability to take up nutrients. If the pH is too high or too low, elements such as phosphorus, one of the important macronutrients for plant health, may be locked up in insoluble compounds and unavailable to plants. In order for plants to be able to gather nutrients through their roots, those nutrients must be in water-soluble form.

The soil can be brought into balance through the use of amendments added when composted matter is worked into the soil. In established gardens, amendments may have to be worked into the soil around individual

Blueberries grow well in acid soil and require plenty of sun and water.

plants. Extension service laboratories offer recommendations for correcting existing soils when they provide the results of the soil tests (see pages 106 and 107).

The pH scale uses 7.0 as a neutral point, with values above being alkaline and values below being acidic. Since it's a logarithmic scale, a soil with a pH of 5.8 is ten times as acid as one with a pH of 6.8. Most garden plants will thrive in soils with a pH in the 6.5 to 7.0 range. Extension service laboratories recommend corrections to a pH of 6.6.

Although the pH can vary considerably from spot to spot in a garden and from season to season depending on rainfall, soil care, and other factors, a test that analyzes soil taken from several places in the garden (see page 21) gives you a fairly definitive reading.

When changing soil pH, consider the soil's composition. Organic soils and heavy, clay soils react more slowly to pH modifiers than do light, sandy soils. The small particles of clay hold, or adsorb, more ions—the electrically charged particles that cause acidity or alkalinity—thus resisting pH changes. A high percentage of

Soil Reaction Chart (pH)

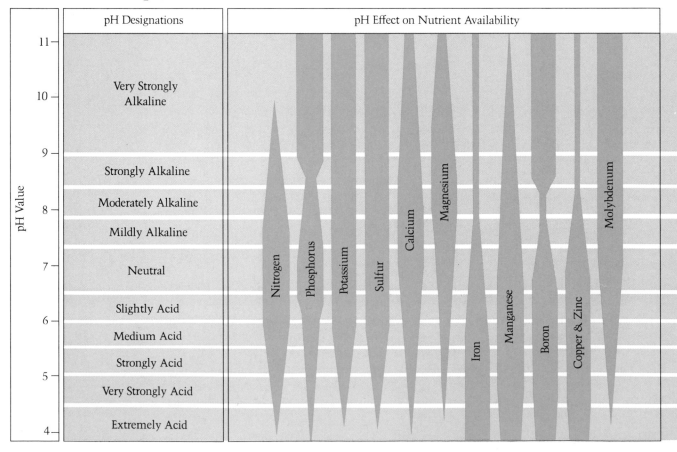

pH Value	pH Designations	pH Effect on Nutrient Availability
11	Very Strongly Alkaline	Nitrogen, Phosphorus, Potassium, Sulfur, Calcium, Magnesium, Iron, Manganese, Boron, Copper & Zinc, Molybdenum
10		
9	Strongly Alkaline	
8	Moderately Alkaline / Mildly Alkaline	
7	Neutral	
6	Slightly Acid / Medium Acid	
5	Strongly Acid / Very Strongly Acid	
4	Extremely Acid	

organic matter in soil buffers the effects of pH modifiers. In both instances, gardeners will have to add more soil modifiers.

Once the soil has been balanced to the right pH for the plants in a specific garden, it should be analyzed every five years, every three years if a lot of fertilizer is applied. If high-analysis fertilizers are used, soil tests should be made annually, since these products increase soil acidity.

Making Acid Soil More Basic

Most ornamentals and vegetables yield less than promised in acid soils. Highly acidic soil, with a pH of 6.0 or less, will not be productive for most plants. Some exceptions are azaleas, rhododendrons, blueberries, cranberries, watermelons, white potatoes, and pineapples.

Lime is mixed into soils to raise its pH level. The most common lime, and the safest to use, is agricultural lime, a ground limestone composed mainly of calcium carbonate. Another good material that supplies magnesium in addition to calcium is dolomitic limestone.

Watermelon grows best in acid soil. If the season is short, select an early-maturing variety.

Soil Reaction Chart (pH)

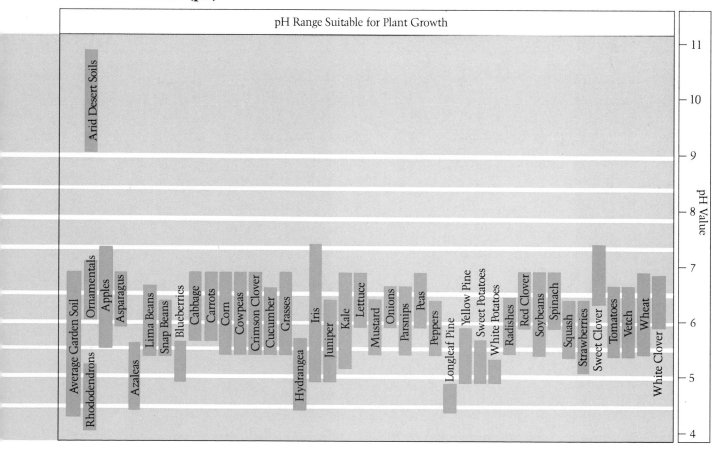

It usually takes about six months from the time that the lime is applied until its full effect on the soil pH is achieved. But in hot weather, it might take only three to four months. Lime is best applied in autumn to get the soil ready for spring planting, or in spring for late crops.

Making Basic Soil More Acid

When soil tests indicate that soils are too sweet, or basic, for growing the plant varieties planned for that garden, steps must be taken to make that soil more acidic and lower the pH nearer to the ideal 6.8.

The use of finely ground sulfur, which has a long residual effect, is a good way to lower soil pH. When the amounts recommended by the soil-testing lab have been applied, two to three months with minimum temperatures of 60° F should produce the desired result.

MULCH

A mulch can be any material placed over the soil to conserve moisture, prevent weed growth, and moderate soil temperatures. Mulches imitate nature by providing soils with a covering. Next to composting, mulching is probably the most important practice a gardener should adopt. With regular mulches, plants can thrive under many adverse conditions.

In the past, all mulches were organic. But more recently, home gardeners have achieved good results with such inorganic mulches as black and clear polyethylene film, colored stones, gravel, and similar materials. But it's the organic mulches that really deserve gardeners' attention. As a product of plants, they return nutrients to the earth and help improve soil structure and texture.

A 2- to 3-inch layer of an organic mulch, the specific amount depending on the material and on the garden situation, also reduces compaction, reduces soil erosion on slopes, protects plants from being heaved out of the soil by winter freeze and thaw cycles, and gives garden beds a finished look. The lighter and more airy the mulch, the thicker it can be applied. Fresh straw, for instance, could be layered 5 to 6 inches thick; finely shredded hardwood bark should be limited to 2 to 3 inches.

A side benefit of mulching is that it keeps overeager mowers and lawn trimmers from wreaking havoc on trees and shrubs. Few gardeners have not had their woody plants damaged by mowing equipment and weed-eaters.

When used under fruit trees and berry bushes, mulches prevent bruising when the ripe fruits drop. Legumes, hays, and grasses, when used as mulches, add considerable amounts of nutrients to the soil as they decay.

Black plastic mulch is not pretty, but it has advantages. It modifies soil temperature, conserves moisture, controls weeds, prevents compaction, and repels insects.

In fact, some experts report that well-mulched fruit trees will outperform others, even if the unmulched trees are fertilized.

Mulches do have a few drawbacks. Hay and straw may attract mice and voles, and some mulches might be fire hazards during dry weather. If high winds are likely in dry periods, be sure that mulch around dwellings is kept moist. This could be a problem in areas where water rationing is prevalent, but, as shown in the next chapter, certain practices can maximize the use of available water.

Dangers of Overmulching

Gardeners should beware of overmulching. Moderation and good sense are the keys. Mulches are not cases of "if a little will do a good job, then a lot will do an even better job."

Overmulching young trees, for example, with a layer 10 inches thick and extending out from 2 to 4 feet around the trunk allows burrowing rodents access to tender, tasty bark, their damage going undiscovered until the tree's foliage begins to die. In addition, excessively deep mulch around the base of young trees often becomes soggy, which encourages growth of soilborne diseases as well as the eventual decay of the tree trunk itself. Finally, the roots of saplings, especially those recently transplanted, are apt to suffocate when covered with soggy mulch because their systems are still comparatively small.

Mulches should be kept pulled away from the base of trees and be applied thin enough to keep them from becoming soggy and preventing air circulation throughout the soil. When mulches are overly rich in nutrients or applied too heavily, they can also inhibit spring growth, encourage growth too late in autumn, and produce poorly colored fruit that drops excessively.

Mulching Tips

To avoid problems such as those described above, follow this general rule for proper mulching: Apply most organic mulches to a depth of only 2 to 3 inches and don't add more until that layer is thin and well decayed.

Apply mulches for summer crops in spring after the soil has warmed. The reason for waiting is that mulch applied too early slows normal plant growth by insulating the soil from the warming sun.

Soil amendments include limestone, compost, wood ash, organic fertilizer, and leaf mold.

Mulching a Tree

Mulch   Weed

Adding a layer of mulch keeps soil moist and makes weeds easy to remove. Leaving a space between the mulch and the tree prevents trunk rot.

How Much Mulch?

This chart shows how many cubic feet of shredded bark would be needed for a 3-inch layer of mulch on garden borders and beds. To use the chart, find the intersections of the columns showing length and width of bed. Bags are usually marked according to the number of cubic feet they contain.

Length of Bed	Width of Bed			
	5'	10'	15'	20'
5'	6.25	12.50	18.75	25
10'	12.50	25.00	37.50	50
15'	18.75	37.50	56.25	75
20'	25	50	75	100

A 3-inch layer of shredded bark or an equivalent mulch should be applied to the ground around trees and shrubs and atop vegetable and ornamental beds. Garden beds can be top-dressed whenever needed. As the season progresses, the organic mulch decomposes gradually, adding nutrients to the soil at the same time as it improves the quality.

Apply a 2- to 3-inch layer of winter mulch to trees, shrubs, and garden beds after the first hard freeze in autumn. Again, this insulates the soil, keeps it from thawing, and prevents freeze-thaw cycles that are destructive to plant tissue. Winter mulch also protects established plants from stressful temperature extremes during this season.

A deep layer of straw keeps soil cool, assuring good lettuce production. Make sure that the straw is seed free or weeds may be a problem.

When mulching with organic materials, keep the following tips in mind.

☐ Avoid placing thick mulch on perennial plant crowns. Mulch around but not on the crown itself to avoid smothering it.

☐ Never plant through dry mulch, especially during hot, dry, windy weather.

☐ Soak mulch before or immediately after applying to gardens. Otherwise, mulch acts like a wick and pulls moisture from tender plant tissue when the weather is hot and dry.

☐ Check mulched beds regularly to see that both the soil and the mulch are moist but not sopping wet.

☐ Add more mulch during the season as the mulch layer decays.

☐ NEVER make mulch from lawn clippings treated with broad-leafed weed controls! These herbicides are harmful to all broad-leafed plants, including trees, shrubs, and flowering annuals and perennials.

Top: Impatiens seedlings flourish in planting mix. Bottom: River rocks around this tree are both a decorative element and a practical mulch.

Soil Amendment Chart
Mulch and Compost

Many of the organic mulches listed here are also likely prospects for the compost pile as long as their texture is fine enough to decompose fairly rapidly and keep from matting. Because some materials are by-products of regional industries, they may not be available in every area.

ORGANIC

Material	Where to Find	Remarks
Bark mulch	Garden centers	Good mulch if shredded
Buckwheat hulls	Garden centers	Long lasting, good color
Cocoa-bean hulls	Candy manufacturers	Good color, long lasting, aromatic
Corncobs (ground)	Corn-growing areas	Good mulch, not very attractive
Cranberry clippings	Cape Cod, Wisconsin	Attractive for acid-loving plants
Hay	Feed stores	Useful in vegetable gardens
Hops (used)	Breweries	Good mulch, odor persists for a time
Lawn clippings	Lawn	If too green, may mat and heat
Leafmold	Composted leaves	Wonderful for woodland flowers
Leaves	Deciduous trees	Better if shredded and composted
Manure	Stables and farms	Better after composting
Mushroom compost	Commercial mushroom growers	Dark color, some nutrient value
Newspaper	Several layers of black-and-white newsprint may be used under a raised bed to separate from previous soil level	When covered with leaves, grass clippings, or shredded bark, newspaper becomes a mulch
Peanut hulls	Southern states	Good mulch but not very attractive
Peat moss	Garden centers	Best when mixed with other matter
Pine needles	Conifers	Attractive, good for wildflower gardens
Salt hay	Near seashores	Good mulch
Sawdust	Sawmills	Good mulch, add nitrogen
Seaweed	Near seashores	Good for mineral elements
Straw	Feed stores	Coarser, longer lasting than hay
Tobacco stems (chopped)	Tobacco farms	Coarse, discourages insects
Wood chips	Tree prunings	Good mulch, coarser than sawdust, less apt to cause nitrogen deficiency

INORGANIC

Material	Remarks
Aluminum foil	May be used under tomato plants, eggplants, and green peppers when they are bothered by insects.
Weed-blocking fabrics	Specially designed plastic fabrics that allow air and water to pass through, but not weeds. Generally covered with organic mulch to improve appearance.
Plastic, black	May be used in vegetable gardens to warm the soil, kill weeds, and discourage further weed growth. Also used under decorative gravels and stones to discourage weed growth.
Plastic, clear	Use like black plastic. Reminder: Clear plastic, like a minigreenhouse, encourages weed germination and growth. Warms the soil. In hot weather, can heat soil to killing temperatures.
Stones, gravel	Decorative, available in many colors and textures. Used for minimal-care areas with high environmental stress, such as parking lots and entryways. Some types good for rock gardens and alpine gardens.

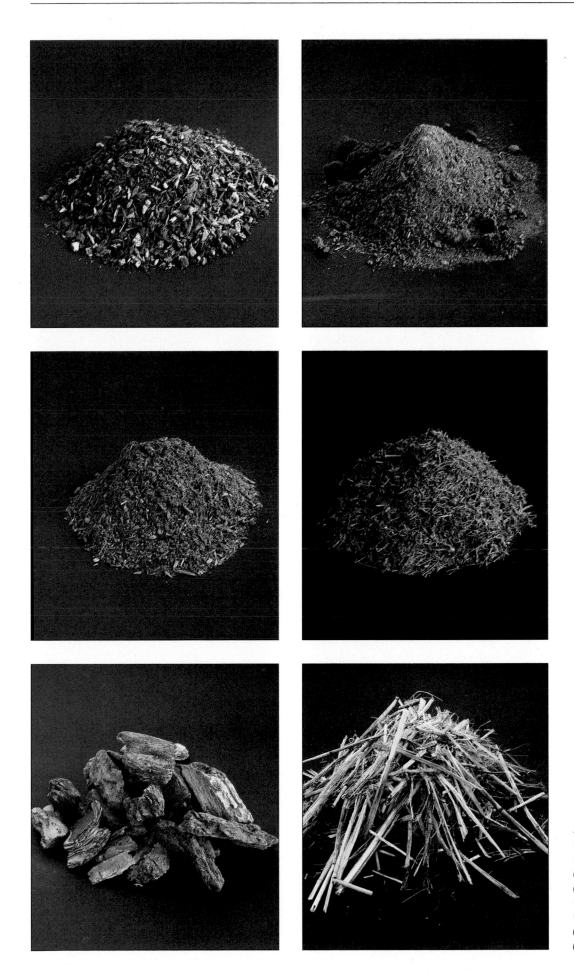

An array of mulches and amendments: fir bark (top left), manure (top right), sawdust (center left), grass clippings (center right), wood chips (bottom left), and hay (bottom right).

A sterile potting mix is all-important for growing seedlings and plants in pots. You can buy it or make your own.

POTTING MIXES

Although the ingredients in potting mixes vary, they are all designed to supply the demands of growing seedlings and cuttings. Mixes support plant growth by supplying nutrients, encouraging proper drainage, and retaining maximum air and moisture needed for root development.

For the small-space gardener who concentrates on growing plants in containers or raised beds, buying synthetic potting mixes has advantages. These prepared commercial mixes are lightweight, easy to use, and free of disease organisms, insects, and weed seeds. However, gardeners who need more than just a few cubic feet of potting mix will find it cheaper to make their own.

Basic Ingredients

Commercial organic mixes contain sphagnum peat moss, shredded bark, wood shavings, or sawdust. Their mineral component may be vermiculite, perlite, pumice, sand, or a combination of these. The mix you buy could be composed of peat moss and vermiculite, ground bark, and fine sand, or some other combination.

Cornell University and the University of California pioneered soilless mixtures. U. C.'s synthetic mixes include sand, peat moss, and shredded bark in varying proportions. Both Cornell's Peat-lite A (half peat moss and half vermiculite) and Peat-lite B (half peat moss and one quarter each vermiculite and perlite) are good for growing seedlings and most other annuals.

A good mixture for encouraging foliage is composed of half peat moss and one quarter each vermiculite and perlite. For such epiphytic plants as orchids and bromeliads, consider a mix with one third each peat moss, perlite, and finely shredded Douglas fir bark.

Making Your Own Mix

Often gardeners prefer to make their own mix. Those with large areas to cover find it more economical to make up batches or add garden topsoil to stretch commercial products. For instance, most plants in containers or hanging baskets are happy with a blend of topsoil and potting soil.

Adding garden soil, however, takes away the advantages of the sterilized mix. Whether you plant seedlings in mix or topsoil, a sprinkling of sphagnum peat moss over the surface helps prevent damping-off, a fungal disease spread by spores in the air.

The mixing process is the same for any formula. Dump the ingredients into a pile and roughly blend them, dampening the mixture as you go. (Dry peat moss is far easier to wet with warm water than with cold.) Sprinkle fertilizer, lime, and other amendments over the pile. Mix the ingredients thoroughly by shoveling from the first pile to a second. To ensure that the ingredients are well mixed, shovel from the second pile to a third. If not used soon after mixing, the mixture can be stored in plastic bags or plastic garbage cans.

Blending small batches of ingredients in a wheelbarrow lets you trundle the mixture directly to the plant site. If the quantities are too large, mix them on a painter's drop cloth or other suitable ground covering.

A good tip when adding planting soil to large, stationary containers such as barrels is to fill the bottom half of the containers with black-and-white newspaper (colored inks are not good for garden soils) before adding 6 to 8 inches of planting mixture. Far less potting soil is needed, and the plant roots have plenty of room to grow.

If you need only a few cubic feet of planting mix, a commercial preparation may be your best buy.

Planting and Maintaining Soil

A regular schedule of soil care and maintenance is as important as initial efforts to improve and prepare garden soil. Well-timed watering, mulching, composting, and fertilizing keep garden soils fertile and plants healthy.

For gardeners who like to get the best results with the least amount of effort, a regular schedule of soil care makes gardening more enjoyable as well as more productive. The initial work of improving garden soil and choosing and setting out plants can represent a major investment of time and money. From that point on, regular maintenance assures a return on that investment.

Choosing the right plants for the specific site and climate also enables the soil to better fill its various roles, helps plants grow more vigorously, and makes gardening less demanding and more successful. Healthy plants resist invasions by pests and disease.

Plant choice is directly related to the amount of water a garden requires. Some plants need much more water than others. This chapter shows gardeners how to use supplemental watering to make up for lack of rainfall. Guidelines explain when to water for best results and how much to use.

Even after the soil is planted with vegetables or ornamentals, it needs regular mulching and composting. Experienced gardeners plan a season or so in advance to have composts and mulches ready to apply at appropriate times.

When to fertilize, what to use, and how much to apply are a part of the sound practices required for a productive garden. Sometimes, plants thrive with little or no attention. When that happy situation occurs, there may be no need to add extra nutrients.

Just how much water does your garden need? It depends on the weather, the season, the soil, and specific plants.

When gardeners can recognize healthy plants, they're ahead of the game. They can look at a bed and tell just which plants are thriving and which may need extra attention. Although the symptoms of plant distress are easy to identify, their exact cause is often harder to pinpoint. As the feature on page 13 shows, disparate causes can result in similar symptoms. This chapter includes information on recognizing plant health, plus reminders of good planting techniques. Recommendations are included for specific plant choices for particular garden situations.

GOOD PLANTING TECHNIQUES

The aim of good planting is to cause as little injury as possible to the root system as well as to the foliage of seedlings and mature plants. The less the root system is disturbed, the quicker the plant will recover from the shock of transplantation and the more rapidly it will begin growing normally.

Even when the root system is lifted and moved with a large and firmly attached amount of soil, it's next to impossible to transplant without injuring some tiny rootlets, but

Work swiftly when transplanting to keep the plant roots from drying out.

For easiest maintenance, a garden site should be properly prepared before planting. Here, the soil is being tilled to improve its structure.

Bare-Root Planting

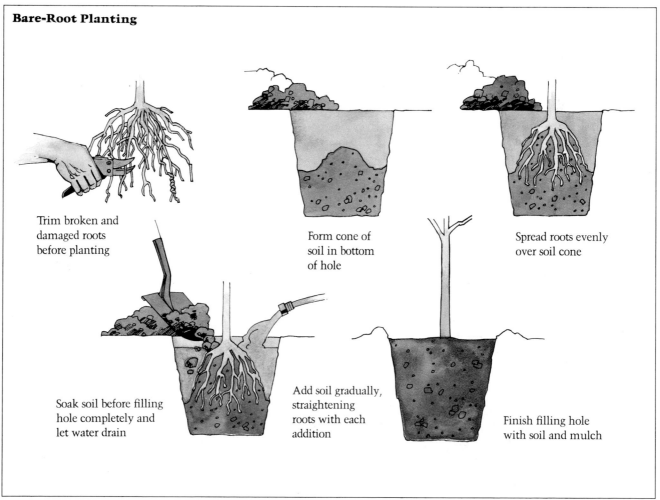

Trim broken and damaged roots before planting

Form cone of soil in bottom of hole

Spread roots evenly over soil cone

Soak soil before filling hole completely and let water drain

Add soil gradually, straightening roots with each addition

Finish filling hole with soil and mulch

When planting balled-and-burlapped shrubs and trees, keep rootballs moist and intact. If you can't plant right away, cover the ball with moist organic matter.

the amount of damage can be minimized. The key is to work firmly and quickly when lifting and moving plants from place to place.

Roots, especially the myriad of root hairs that carry on the actual work of taking in air, water, and nutrients, should never be allowed to dry out completely. If they do, their ability to function properly will be greatly diminished, threatening the plant's existence.

The soil in the garden bed should be prepared prior to planting (see the chapter titled "Preparing the Soil," starting on page 33). The soil should be cultivated when neither too dry nor too wet, and both soil and mulch should be moist when plants are installed. If the soil and mulch are too dry, they may cause moisture to be pulled out of tender plant tissues.

Planting Tips

For the reasons mentioned above, planting chores are best done on calm days when it is neither too hot nor too cold. A cloudy day is far better for planting than a sunny one; freshly

---

Planting From a Container

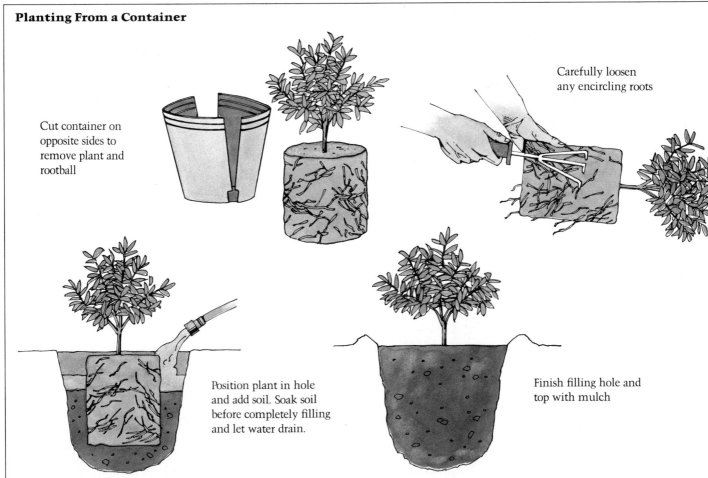

Cut container on opposite sides to remove plant and rootball

Carefully loosen any encircling roots

Position plant in hole and add soil. Soak soil before completely filling and let water drain.

Finish filling hole and top with mulch

planted seedlings are very susceptible to losing moisture by transpiration. Moisture lost directly through the pores in the foliage causes the plant to wilt. Injured roots may not be able to replace water fast enough to avoid deprivation in the plant tissues.

Experienced gardeners are speedy when transplanting seedlings. They have the new site prepared and have assembled all the tools and materials they will need before beginning work. Once they pop the seedlings out of their pots, the plants are in the ground in their new location in a very short time, leaving the roots exposed to the drying atmosphere only briefly.

Planting holes for shrubs and trees should be just as deep as the rootball and twice as wide. It's better to place woody plants, trees, and shrubs into holes a bit too shallow rather than too deep.

The soil from the planting hole does not need to be greatly improved before being used as backfill, especially if the native soil is heavy and clayey. If the planting hole soil has a far better texture and structure than the surrounding soil, roots will not spread out and a "clay-pot" effect is created. When that happens, water collects in the improved soil instead of draining into the surrounding soil, and plants may drown because air can't circulate properly.

If planting must be delayed, there are a few techniques that will help protect plant roots from drying out. Shrubs, trees, and other sizable plants can be heeled in—put into a temporary spot where the rootballs can be covered with moist soil or the equivalent. Rootballs of large plants can also be kept covered with a moist tarpaulin. If smaller plants have already been popped out of their pots, layer them close together and cover lightly with moist newspaper or cloth.

When to Plant

New gardeners often ask what seasons are best for planting and transplanting. Although container plants can be set out any time the soil can be worked, tender plants should not be put into garden beds until the ground has warmed up, well after the last hard frost. Plant roots will grow as long as the soil temperature is above 40° F.

Spring is the traditional season for planting shrubs, trees, and perennials, but as long as proper care is given after transplanting, almost any season will do. Autumn offers one advantage over spring: Plants set out then stand a better chance of providing a good showing the following summer.

For additional information on the best planting seasons, check with garden centers,

---

Soil Temperatures And Plant Growth

Plant growth depends not only on the physical qualities of the soil and the environmental aspects of the garden site, but also on the soil temperature. The following is a list of minimum soil temperatures required to grow certain vegetable crops. Buying an inexpensive probe-type soil thermometer is a good investment for keeping track of soil temperatures.

Minimum Soil Temperature	Plants
32° F	Onion, spinach, parsnip
40° F	Radish, carrot, beet, cabbage, pea
50° F	Corn, asparagus, tomato
60° F	Squash, cucumber, bean, pepper, melon

Seedlings can be thinned or transplanted as soon as they have acquired true leaves.

Apply chemical fertilizers exactly as instructed on the label. Too much fertilizer can burn tender young plants.

state extension services, or public gardens. Also note the feature on minimum soil temperature for vegetable growth on page 59.

FERTILIZER

To increase plant growth and production, fertilizers are added to the soil. Some fertilizers are manufactured; some are natural by-products. The most important thing to remember when adding fertilizer is to read the label carefully and to follow the directions precisely.

Too much fertilizer can often be worse than none at all. As is true with overmulching and overwatering, a too-generous application of fertilizer can damage or kill plants. It's better to err on the side of caution. Compare fertilizing to adding salt to soup. The good cook checks the recipe to make sure that the right amount is being used. Experience and judgment are important factors.

At one time, commercial farmers would grow crops on the same piece of land for years. When the land wore out, they moved to a new section. They had a big choice of acreage in America's rich grain and corn belt. Those immense prairies and plains boasted organic-rich,

well-structured soils, thanks to the incorporation of organic plant materials that dated back millions of years.

After the farmers worked the land for several years, the soil nutrients and organic components were depleted and not replaced. In fact, it was only recently that agricultural experts and soil scientists learned the importance of maintaining and improving soils.

Now we know that it is particularly important to fertilize and maintain soils after vegetables, grains, and other crops have been harvested. And, although ornamentals usually do not remove as many nutrients from the garden in the normal growing season, proper soil maintenance assures maximum productivity.

Types of Fertilizer

Gardeners and manufacturers separate fertilizers into two main types, organic and inorganic. Organic fertilizers include manures, plant by-products, and other materials produced by natural means. Inorganic fertilizers are manufactured substances whose mineral salts and plant nutrients are produced from industrial processes. These fertilizers are usually referred to as chemical fertilizers.

In truth, many of the chemical fertilizers are organic in the scientific sense of the word since they contain carbon. But the important thing to remember about fertilizers is that the plants neither care nor differentiate between the use of natural nutrients and those produced industrially.

One advantage of using chemical fertilizers is that far less of the material is needed to add the required amount of nutrients to the soil. For example, a ton of cow manure would have to be used to gain the same amount of nitrogen found in 50 pounds of 20-20-20 fertilizer.

Much of the objection to chemical fertilizers can be traced to their overuse on soils whose structure had not been previously improved. That resulted in tremendous runoff of excess fertilizers into streams, rivers, and lakes.

Both commercial farmers and home gardeners tend to overuse fertilizers. Seeking proper soil testing and following the laboratories' accurate recommendations for correcting any deficiencies could help prevent this overuse.

Organic fertilizer The advantage of using natural organic fertilizers, such as well-rotted manure, fish meal, compost, and peat moss, is that these materials offer more than nutrients. Although compost and peat moss are not classified strictly as fertilizers, they provide nutrient value in addition to their primary function as soil enhancers. They also contain organic fibrous matter that helps improve the structure of soils.

Organic fertilizers include sizable percentages of undecomposed plant and animal remains, which are valuable for amending both the texture and structure of soils. These well-structured soils retain more nutrients and water and allow better air circulation. The more the soil structure is improved, the less fertilizer is required.

Processed organic fertilizers include not only composted manures but also some rock minerals.

Inorganic (chemical) fertilizer These fertilizers have the advantages of being very precise. Their analyses are printed on the container labels, so that the fertilizer can be matched exactly to the plant's specific needs.

Chemical fertilizers are readily available and easy to apply, an advantage for inexperienced gardeners. They can be purchased in many sizes, from small containers to large bags and even in bulk. This eliminates the often difficult storage problem for those whose space is limited.

Because chemical fertilizers are so precise and concentrated, gardeners must learn to read the labels carefully (see the feature on page 62) and use good judgment when adding them to garden soils. Some fertilizers can burn plant tissue if too much is used or if they are applied improperly. Fertilizer burn is caused by concentrated particles contacting plant tissue, injurious fumes from volatile fertilizers, or an accumulation of mineral salts in the ground during periods of drought.

It should be noted that injuries from "hot" fertilizers can happen with uncomposted manure as well as with the use of too much chemical fertilizer.

Fertilizer Requirements

Different plants require different levels of fertilizing. Since home gardeners usually grow a variety of plants, they need to know the relative fertilizer needs of the plant. Generally speaking, the following plant groups have high, medium, or low needs for the primary nutrients of nitrogen, phosphorus, and potassium.

Vegetables	High
Fruits	Medium
Herbs	Low to medium
Lawns	Medium to high
Annual flowers	Medium
Perennial flowers	Medium to low
Deciduous trees and shrubs	Medium to low
Evergreen trees and shrubs	Low

The numbers on fertilizer containers represent the amounts of nitrogen (N), phosphorus (P), and potassium (K)—the main nutrients needed by plants—contained in the product.

An excellent soil conditioner, compost is often used as an organic fertilizer.

The N-P-K numbers refer to the pounds of those elements by percentages in each 100 pounds of fertilizer. The amounts of other nutrients in fertilizer mixes are listed in minimum percentages on the labels.

Fertilizer nitrogen is found in a number of compounds. Phosphorus in fertilizers is found as the compound phosphoric acid (P_2O_5). Potassium is found as the compound potash (K_2CO_3).

Nitrogen is the element most often in short supply, since plants use so much of it and it's easily leached out of the soil by water. Lack of adequate nitrogen is one of the easiest things to spot in a garden. The plant-symptom chart on page 13 describes the typical symptoms of such nutrient deficiencies.

The larger the N number on the container, the less will be needed for a given area. In the chart below you see how the amount to be applied decreases as the percentage of nitrogen increases (the percentage of nitrogen is indicated by the first number in each series).

When to Apply

The results of a soil test include recommendations for adding nutrients that are in poor supply. These recommendations usually include timing of fertilizer applications as well.

Generally, gardeners apply fertilizers when the plants are growing, the time they need the most nutrients. If you live in a cold-winter area, it's wise to stop fertilizing gardens at the end of summer. Late fertilizing encourages growth that would be too young and tender to withstand winter stress.

Vegetables and flowers are generally fertilized on a regular basis throughout the season. Spring-flowering bulbs should be fertilized early in the season so that they can have ample nutrients for developing the following year's blossoms.

There are several schools of thought about how often lawns should be fertilized. Some experts recommend fertilizing cool-weather lawns, including bluegrass and fescue, in the autumn, spring, and also during the growing season. Others say to fertilize only in autumn; they believe that warm-weather fertilizing of cool-weather turf encourages weeds. Fertilizing warm-weather turfgrasses, such as zoysiagrass and bermudagrass, during the summer encourages growth—and mowing.

---

1 **General Purpose Plant Food**

2 **8-8-8**

3 **Guaranteed Analysis:**

4 Total Nitrogen (N)   8%

5
- 3.1% Ammoniacal Nitrogen
- 1.2% Urea Nitrogen
- 2.4% Nitrate Nitrogen
- 1.3% Water Insoluble Nitrogen

6 Available Phosphoric Acid (P_2O_5)   8%

7 Soluble Potash (K_2CO_3)   8%

8 Primary Nutrients from Ammonium Sulfate, Urea, Ammonium Phosphates, Sulfate of Potash, and Muriate of Potash

9
Calcium (Ca)	1.5%
Magnesium (Mg)	1.0%
Sulfur (S)	4.5%
Iron (Fe)	0.2%
Manganese (Mn)	0.08%
Zinc (Zn)	0.09%

10 Secondary and Trace Nutrients from Dolomitic Limestone, Ammonium Sulfate, Sulfate of Potash, Iron Sulfate, Manganese Oxide, and Zinc Oxide

11 Potential Acidity 400 lbs. Calcium Carbonate Equivalent per ton

1) In this example, "General Purpose Plant Food" is the equivalent of a brand name. **2)** The formula, grade, or analysis, these numbers are the percentages of nitrogen, phosphate, and potash (always in that order) of the contents. **3)** The manufacturer's warranty that the stated analysis is present in the container. The guaranteed analysis is always stated in this order and form. **4)** This is the sum total of the percentages of nitrogen from the listed sources. **5)** These percentages are not required in every case, but most manufacturers supply this information. The source of the nitrogen is important because, in many respects, the source governs the way the nitrogen reacts in the soil. **6 & 7)** The percentages of the other two primary nutrients are listed only if their presence is claimed elsewhere on the label. **8)** The sources of the three primary nutrients. In most cases, the sources are basic fertilizers which, when combined, make a "complete" fertilizer. **9)** Percentages of secondary nutrients and micronutrients may be present in fertilizers but not always claimed on the label. If percentages are indicated, the manufacturer guarantees those amounts. **10)** Sources of secondary nutrients and micronutrients. **11)** Some fertilizers have an acid reaction in the soil. If this potential exists, the label will indicate the number of pounds of calcium carbonate (laboratory quality limestone) it would take to completely neutralize the acidity of the fertilizer once it was in the soil.

Fertilizer Formulas

Formula	Pounds Per 100 Square Feet*
5-10-10	3.5
6-18-6	2.8
8-24-8	2.0
12-6-6	1.4
16-16-16	1.0

* If a liquid fertilizer is used, convert the recommendations made for dry fertilizer into pints or cups: 1 pint fertilizer weighs about 1 pound; 1 cup weighs about ½ pound.

Top: Celery grows best in fertilizer-enriched soil. Liquid fertilizer added to irrigation water every two to three weeks encourages growth. Bottom: Covering a perennial bed with a layer of mulch protects it against frost.

Complete and Single-Nutrient Fertilizers

Fertilizers come in many forms. Classifications may include the words *complete* and *single-nutrient,* broad terms that refer to nutrients contained in the fertilizer. Complete fertilizers include all three macronutrients (nitrogen, phosphorus, and potassium); incomplete fertilizers contain only one or two. Fertilizers referred to as balanced include equal amounts by weight percentages of the three major nutrients; unbalanced fertilizers contain unequal amounts. Single-nutrient fertilizers include only one of these major elements.

An example of a complete fertilizer is one with the N-P-K numbers 5-10-5, showing that all three macronutrients are present in the formula. A fertilizer with 5-5-5 on the label is not only complete but balanced, containing the same percentages by weight of all three major nutrients. One example of a single-nutrient fertilizer is 0-20-0, the formula for superphosphate, an excellent source of phosphorus.

Complete fertilizers are meant for general use; incomplete formulas are used to treat specific deficiencies. Balanced fertilizers are used generally; unbalanced ones are often recommended for specific plant groups. Fertilizers high in nitrogen (always the first number listed) are good for foliage plants, including turfgrasses. Fertilizers high in the second two numbers, phosphorus and potassium, are good for flowering and fruiting plants.

Single-nutrient fertilizers correct certain deficiencies or meet special needs of plants. Superphosphate, for instance, is a nutrient often recommended for bulbous plants.

Fast- and Slow-Release Fertilizers

Fertilizers are also classified as either fast release or slow release. These terms refer primarily to the nitrogen availability of the formula. Fast-release fertilizers include nitrogen in the form of water-soluble nitrates.

Ammonium nitrate (NH_4NO_3), calcium nitrate ($Ca(NO_3)_2$), and potassium nitrate (KNO_3) are the most common forms used in gardens, with ammonium nitrate the one most often found. Nitrogen in this form is easily available to plants, but, because it's water soluble, it's easily washed out of the soil.

Slow-release fertilizers are those with the highest percentage of the nitrogen in forms that are not water soluble. Controlled-release, or slow-release, fertilizers are good choices for sandy soils and areas with high rainfall, because they slow down the leaching of nitrogen from the soil. The speed of conversion of water-insoluble nitrogen to usable nitrogen (water-soluble salts) in the soil is greatest in soils with high microorganism activity.

Slow-release fertilizer comes in pellet form, which makes nitrogen available over a comparatively long period of time, and in controlled- or time-release capsules covered with resin membranes that dissolve slowly. Ureaform (also known as ureas-form or methaline urea), another type of slow-release fertilizer, is a chemically modified form of urea, an important source of nitrogen. Advantages of this slow-release source of nitrogen are twofold: It will not burn plants, and it contains 35 to 40 percent nitrogen, some 70 percent of which is water insoluble.

Spikes and stakes are a newer form of slow-release fertilizers. Usually only 2 to 3 inches long, they are made from a fiber impregnated with fertilizer. Inserted in the soil around a plant's root area, they slowly release nitrogen

A root feeder applies nutrients directly to the root zone of trees and large shrubs.

and other nutrients as the fiber disintegrates. How often they must be replaced depends largely on whether the fertilizer is a slow-release or fast-release type.

Handy for use around trees and shrubs as well as for house plants and container plantings, this form of fertilizer is expensive for larger gardening projects.

Other Fertilizer Forms

In addition to the pellets and spikes described above, fertilizers come in liquid, powdered, and granular forms. Both the liquid and powdered fertilizers provide fast solutions for plant nutrient deficiency disorders, but both tend to leach from the soil and must be applied more frequently than granular fertilizer.

Concentrated liquid fertilizers must be diluted with water before application. They are very convenient to use in small gardens and container plantings but may be impractical for large areas.

Powdered fertilizers must be dissolved in water before application. They are not as easy to store as liquid forms, since they may cake over time.

A hose-end sprayer distributes a preset mixture of liquid fertilizer and water onto plants.

A hand-held broadcast spreader applies dry fertilizer accurately to small areas.

Ready-to-Use Containers

Small containers of liquid fertilizer may include spray applicators along with directions for spraying foliage or soil. This is a handy way to fertilize small gardens and container plants.

Hose-End Sprayers

These sprayers apply liquid fertilizer through nozzles that regulate the output and settings that automatically mix the recommended ratio of fertilizer to water. They attach to garden hoses and offer several spray patterns.

Fine sprays cover both tops and undersides of leaves. Solid streams reach the upper branches of plants up to 25 feet high. Heavy, drenching sprays apply materials that need to be washed into the soil, such as insecticides and liquid fertilizers. Specialized hose-end sprayers are available with elongated nozzles to spray the tops of trees and inside the dense foliage of shrubs and hedges.

Tips for Use

1. Follow specific directions for application.
2. Select the spray pattern by rotating the nozzle to the desired position. If your sprayer has a dial, set it to the dilution rate specified on the label.
3. Clean the applicator as instructed. Never leave leftover product in the unit.

Broadcast Spreaders

These tools distribute granular fertilizers, as well as grass seed and pesticides. They are very useful for spreading fertilizer on landscaped beds, vegetable gardens, and other large areas with uneven surfaces.

Broadcast spreaders consist of a hopper, an agitator, and a spinning disk. The hopper holds the fertilizer. As the gardener begins walking, material moves down through the agitator onto the spinning disk, which broadcasts it in a uniform arc from 4 to 12 feet wide. A micrometer metering control adjusts the amount of fertilizer or other material to be dispensed.

Tips for Use

1. Don't spill fertilizers or other chemical materials on turf or garden areas. Always fill the spreader in a paved or other work area.
2. Read the label to determine the correct spreader setting. The settings are based on a normal walking pace.

Granular fertilizers are usually used in the top- and side-dressing of garden beds and plants. The granules are larger than those found in powdered fertilizers and smaller than the pelletized form. Their nutrients are released as the granules break down in the presence of water. This type of fertilizer is easily spread by hand or with a commercial applicator.

Trionized fertilizer, a comparatively recent development, includes granules of lightweight material, such as vermiculite, to which each of the three major nutrients have been bonded. Every granule of this extremely homogenous fertilizer contains nitrogen, phosphorus, and potassium.

APPLYING FERTILIZER

Although fertilizers can be applied by hand or with a watering can, using a commercial applicator may often be far easier. These calibrated applicators make it easier for home gardeners to prepare and apply the prescribed amounts of fertilizer. If spreading fertilizer by hand, make sure that it is in a form that will not burn the skin on contact.

A fertilizer drop spreader is a fast and easy-to-use applicator for an average-sized lawn.

3. Make passes with the fertilizer applicator along the length of the area rather than the width. Overlap the swaths by 2 to 3 feet.
4. Always shut off the spreader when making sharp turns and bringing the spreader to a complete stop. Never open the spreader while pulling it backward.
5. Follow directions when cleaning the applicator. Never leave fertilizer or other products in the applicator.
6. CAUTION! If the broadcast spreader is also being used for weed killers, make sure that it's washed thoroughly before being used for fertilizing.

Drop Spreaders

Designed to apply granular fertilizers, insecticides, and grass seed on small to medium-sized lawns and gardens, drop spreaders distribute materials in a path as wide as the opening on the bottom of the spreader. The spreader is composed of a hopper, an agitator bar, and the shutoff blade.

Tips for Use
1. Fill the applicator off the lawn to prevent burning the grass.
2. Open the hopper after beginning walking.
3. Close the hopper on turns.

4. Overlap wheel marks on adjacent passes.
5. Calibrate the spreader occasionally to make sure that it is dropping the right amount of fertilizer. Read the instructions on both the fertilizer container and the applicator.

Tractor Pull Spreaders

Some broadcast spreaders attach to riding lawn mowers or tractors for easy application of fertilizers, pesticides, and grass seed on large gardens and lawns. A spinning disk throws material in a 6- to 16-foot-wide arc across the area. A micrometer setting regulates the disk movement as well as the dispense rate of granular fertilizers and grass seed.

Tips for Use
1. Fill the hopper on the sidewalk or driveway to avoid accidentally spilling material on the lawn.
2. Determine the spreader setting from the product label, based on a normal walking pace.
3. Operate the spreader lengthwise on the lawn, with 2- to 3-foot overlapping swaths.
4. Shut off the spreader when making sharp turns and before coming to a complete stop to avoid dumping extra fertilizer.
5. Hose off the spreader after each use; occasionally lubricate the moving parts.

Hand-Held Broadcast Spreaders

These efficient and accurate multipurpose spreaders are designed for fertilizing lawns, ground covers, landscaped beds, and vegetable gardens and for seeding small lawn areas. The spreader is basically a hopper with a crank handle and broadcast wheel. The gardener should walk at a comfortable, even pace, turning the handle one complete turn for each step forward with the right foot. Settings adjust for different kinds of fertilizer or seed.

Tips for Use

1. Apply the product evenly over the area to be treated, walking at a normal pace. Ensure complete coverage by spreading the product in a crisscross pattern, applying a second application at a right angle to the first.

2. Apply a uniform swath 8 to 12 feet wide, noting the width of the first swath and judging the return accordingly. The higher the spreader is held, the wider the swath.

USING MULCH AND COMPOST

Mulching topsoil with organic matter during the growing season suppresses weeds and improves texture.

Preparing the soil and planting the garden are major accomplishments. Once this has been done, a program of regular soil maintenance

will keep the garden productive and help ensure vigorous and healthy plants. An added bonus that comes from regular composting and mulching is that weeding is easier because of the improved soil texture and reduced seed germination.

Organic mulches should be applied to the soil surface whenever the existing mulch begins to disappear. If shredded bark is used, the layer of mulch should be maintained at a depth of 2 to 3 inches. If using a lighter, airier mulch, such as straw or hay, the layer can be thicker.

A garden fork or shovel lifts and spreads mulch nicely. A flathead rake, the kind with rigid steel tines, will help spread the layer evenly. If bags or containers are too heavy to move easily around the garden, transport bulk mulch conveniently in a wheelbarrow, garden cart, or buckets.

Once compost has been worked into the soil, it builds up reserves for plants to draw upon. It's a simple task to work more compost into annual flower and vegetable beds, since these gardens are replanted each year. An additional ½- to 3-inch-thick layer of compost can be spread and worked into the soil each spring or autumn when the beds are idle. Use a garden fork or spade to work the compost about 6 to 8 inches into the soil. A rotary tiller makes this work go even faster.

The best time for adding compost to soil is about a month before planting. If it's added closer to planting time, the compost texture should be finer so that it decomposes faster. If the compost pile is not finished and still has a lot of fibrous matter, it can be worked into the soil in the autumn. By spring, it should be nicely rotted and blended.

When gardens are left empty for a season or more, it's wise to keep a layer of mulch on the surface of the soil to diminish any possible erosion. Wind, rain, and runoff from ice and snow can wreak havoc on unprotected soil, especially on slopes.

If mulches and composts are well decomposed in autumn but are not going to be used until spring, the piles should be covered and kept in a protected spot. When a pile is finished in summer, it should be kept moist until used.

Add compost to established, planted beds by spreading a layer on the soil surface when the existing mulch layer is thin. There's no need to worry about compost being near plant roots or

Fertilizers and Commercial Soil Amendments

The following are a few of the more common fertilizers and soil amendments with a general description of their function in improving soil. In addition to those listed, garden centers have a full range of liquid fertilizers and other specially formulated mixtures for plant groups such as roses, tomatoes, evergreens, bulbs, ferns and ivy, citrus, and avocados. Always check the label carefully and follow the directions for applying fertilizers.

Substance	Guaranteed Analysis	General Description
Aluminum sulfate	100% hydrated aluminum sulfate	Soil amendment; makes soils more acid. Beneficial for acid-loving plants (azaleas, camellias, gardenias, rhododendrons, hydrangeas, orchids, ixora, hibiscus, etc.).
Superphosphate 0-20-0	20% phosphorus	Rich source of phosphorus, one of the primary plant nutrients; helps build sturdy root systems and new tissue, aids in formation of blooms and fruit.
Blood meal 12-0-0	12% nitrogen	Natural, organic source of long-lasting, slow-release nitrogen. For best results, scatter evenly on soil, rake into top 1 to 2 inches, and water thoroughly.
Bonemeal 0-12-0	12% available phosphorus	Phosphorus obtained from bonemeal for use as an organic supplement. Since element does not move much in soil, incorporate meal to a depth of 6 to 8 inches. Do not use for acid-loving plants.
Garden lime	Agricultural lime is primarily calcium carbonate; other garden limes include calcium, magnesium, and their compounds.	Raises pH of acid soil. Faster acting than agricultural limestone, this finely ground horticultural hydrated lime supplies calcium and magnesium, helps loosen clay soil, sweetens compost piles, improves nutrient availability, and reduces toxicity from aluminum. Recommended for use in vegetable gardens, flower beds, lawns, and compost piles.
General purpose plant food 10-10-10	10% nitrogen, 10% phosphorus, 10% potassium	Fertilizer for listed flowers, roses, shrubs, trees, and lawns. Supplies equal amounts of major nutrients. For best results, water immediately after application to dissolve pellets and carry fertilizer into root zone.
General purpose plant food 16-16-16	16% nitrogen, 16% phosphorus, 16% potassium	A highly concentrated formula containing equal amounts of major nutrients. Pelletized, easy to apply with a spreader. For use on trees, shrubs, evergreens, roses, flowers, and vegetables.
Azalea, camellia, and rhododendron food 10-7-7	10% nitrogen, 7% phosphorus, 7% potassium, 3% sulfur	Fertilizer designed for acid-loving plants. Major nutrients plus sulfur for acidifying soil. Label may list acid-loving plants.
Vegetable food 8-10-8	8% nitrogen, 10% phosphorus, 8% potassium	Fertilizer specially formulated for vegetables and strawberries to produce sturdy plants with vigorous root systems, healthy green leaves, abundant flowers, and high-quality produce. Work into soil at planting time and also use later in the season to side-dress plantings.

foliage, because it won't burn the plants. Work it into the top few inches of topsoil, taking care not to injure shallow roots.

Once the annual or semiannual application of compost is in the soil, mulch should be spread on the surface. In cooler parts of the country, this is easier to do during spring or autumn when deciduous plants are leafless.

WATER AND THE GARDEN

In a cooling process called transpiration, water enters plants through their roots and evaporates through the plant's leaves. If more water evaporates than is brought in, as often happens on hot, windy days, the plant wilts.

A lack of water limits plant development during a growing season. Without enough water,

Watering can be fun with a hose-end extender and a pair of bright red boots.

plants become limp, unable to stay erect. Too little water over an extended period causes the green foliage to turn yellow. A vegetable garden suffering from lack of water produces dwarfed plants with stunted roots. The results of such deprivation are very obvious in root crops, such as beets, carrots, and turnips.

Plant foliage contains an average of 75 percent water. Fast-growing root tips and branch tips include even more, as much as 90 to 95 percent. They need this water in their tissues in order for photosynthesis, their main metabolic process, to take place.

Some plants need much more water than others. Gardeners who live where rainfall is scarce and supplemental water is rationed would be well advised to search for plant varieties that require little water.

Water in Soil

Soils must contain water if plant roots are to grow. This moisture is also necessary for holding soluble nutrients, the only form that plant roots can use. Water carries these dissolved nutrients to the roots. This is the major way that plants get nitrogen and the only way that they can take up phosphorus and sulfur.

The amount of water in the soil also affects microscopic life. Many beneficial soil organisms depend on soil moisture. Yet too much water in the soil is as bad as too little; it results in a loss of air, and both microorganic activity and root growth cease.

Soils act as reservoirs, taking up and holding enough water for plant needs through rainfall and supplemental watering. When soils are amended with organic matter, their capacity for soaking up and storing water increases.

Different soil types have differing capacities for water storage. After watering, an average loamy soil may contain as much as 25 percent water, about half of which would be available to plant roots. Sandy soils, which have little storage capacity, soak up water fast but allow it to run through too quickly. Clay soils take up water reluctantly and drain much too slowly.

Water moves in all directions in the soil: up, down, or sideways, toward areas that are less moist. In uniformly textured and structured soils, moisture moves from wet to dry areas. This means that on sunny, hot, or windy days, water evaporates rapidly from the soil surface, causing deeper soil moisture to move to the surface, where it too evaporates.

The speed with which water moves through soil is largely dependent on the size of the pores, those spaces between soil granules. When the soil is compacted, the pore spaces are made smaller and the movement of water is greatly restricted.

Other factors affecting water movement include the amount of organic matter, amount of water already present, and depth of the soil. The rate of water movement also relates to the soil temperature; it moves faster through warm soils. Mulching greatly reduces evaporation.

Water Sources

Knowing the major sources of area water and learning to make the most of what is available are sound garden practices. They help a gardener decide what kinds of plants to grow.

Rainfall, irrigation systems, and surface and underground water sources provide the moisture needed for gardening. Rainfall is a variable

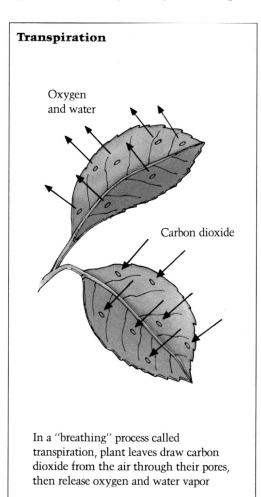

Transpiration

Oxygen and water

Carbon dioxide

In a "breathing" process called transpiration, plant leaves draw carbon dioxide from the air through their pores, then release oxygen and water vapor

blessing, as can be seen on the map on page 103. Even the parts of the country that normally get plenty of rain may have periods of drought.

Irrigation has come to be an important source of water in drier areas. The Colorado River supplies much of the Southwest through a vast system of canals and ditches. In California's large Central Valley, irrigation water may come from miles away. The Mississippi River system, which drains a large portion of the Midwest and West, is another rich source of irrigation water.

Surface and underground water sources depend on lakes and rivers and the drilling of wells that tap into underground reservoirs, called aquifers. The latter is the most expensive form of watering.

Conserving Water

Gardeners can reduce soil water loss by choosing drought-tolerant plants, using mulches, and shading the garden area. Mulches act as barriers to water loss and at the same time cool summer soils by covering the surface.

Choosing plants that require less water is a new gardening direction called xeriscaping. The term comes from the word *xeric,* meaning low or deficient in moisture. A xerophyte is a plant adapted for growing in areas with limited water supplies.

The relationship between soil and climate is close. The hotter the climate, the more rain or supplemental water is needed to sustain plant growth. Conversely, the colder the climate, the less moisture is required. When soils are kept moist in hot climates, both microbial activity and oxidation rates are high. This means that these soils require regular additions of organic matter to be productive.

In the desert regions of the Southwest, homeowners have long been used to rigging systems for the collection and storage of rainwater. As other parts of the country experience drought coupled with an increasing demand for water and dwindling supplies, a need for more irrigation systems has arisen.

For some time, gardeners in these water-short parts of the country have used wastewater for irrigation. This gray water, which comes from the rinse cycles of dishwashers and washing machines or from bathroom tubs and basins, can be used around nonfood crops.

Gardeners concerned about the effects of the increased amount of sodium from water softeners on soil and plants discovered that the addition of gypsum directly to the soil maintained the good soil structure that long-term applications of gray water tended to destroy. Follow manufacturer's instructions concerning the amounts to apply.

Efficient watering systems help conserve water. Chief among these is drip irrigation, which distributes water directly to the root areas of individual plants by means of hoses or flexible tubes with perforations or emitters that drip water slowly into the soil. Drip irrigation eliminates wasteful runoff, minimizes evaporation, and provides water only to the root zones.

Watering Methods

Basically, there are three ways to distribute water to a garden—by sprinkling, flooding, or through drip irrigation. Each of these watering methods has benefits and drawbacks.

Drip Irrigation

Flexible tube with individual emitters distributes water directly to plant roots

Sprinkling Plants that live in cool, rainy climates respond particularly well to this overhead application of water. In warmer areas, plants may appreciate having their foliage washed occasionally. Sprinkling can waste water unless irrigation is timed for early morning or late afternoon to minimize evaporation and wind loss. Sprinkler heads should be carefully placed for best use.

Flooding This method of irrigation, which does exactly what it says, is particularly valuable for directing large amounts of water into basins around deeply rooted trees and large shrubs. It's also useful for watering long rows of vegetables.

Drip irrigation As discussed previously, this system of hoses or flexible tubing that distributes water directly to a plant's roots is valuable in areas where water is in short supply. It also has the added advantage of keeping moisture off lower leaves of plants that might be affected by mold or other diseases, but it's not well suited for watering expanses of lawn.

Watering Techniques

The aim of watering is to supplement inadequate rainfall and conduct moisture to a plant's root zone. How often to water and how much to use are the questions most asked by gardeners.

A rule of thumb that all gardeners should follow is that when you water, water well. This

Evaluating Watering Systems

The decision as to what type of water distribution best serves a gardener's needs depends on the climate and the specific garden—including the plantings and the gardener's time, budget, and philosophy. Some people view watering as a pastime, an opportunity to wander through the garden. If the truth be known, many adults use sprinkling as an excuse to play in water.

Buckets and watering cans	*Pluses:* Least expensive, convenient for mixing liquid fertilizers, handy for small areas and container gardens. *Minuses:* Limited amounts of water at one time, best used in small areas, labor intensive.
Hoses, hose-end nozzles, sprinklers, and attachments such as wands, deep-root irrigators, quick-connect couplers, and timers	*Pluses:* Comparatively inexpensive, distribute water where needed. *Minuses:* Moving hoses to new locations somewhat labor intensive, can waste water if not attended to properly.
Underground sprinkler system	*Pluses:* Can be fully automated with timer, easy to water lawn areas regularly, excellent in areas with adequate water supply. *Minuses:* Usually needs professional installation and maintenance, comparatively expensive, can waste water if not operated wisely.
Drip irrigation systems	*Pluses:* Efficiently bring water slowly and evenly to planted areas and root zones, minimize evaporation and deliver water in prescribed amounts and rates, cut water waste. *Minuses:* Can be complicated to assemble, are more useful for vegetable gardens than ornamental plantings, in areas with hard water (alkaline water with high pH) may be difficult to keep unclogged, must have antisiphon backflow preventers where a system is higher than faucet to prevent contamination of home water supply.
Soaker hose systems	*Pluses:* Newer types made from recycled rubber let water seep out of entire length; provide water to root area rather than foliage, which helps prevent fungal diseases. Result in less runoff, can be buried and used as permanent installation by homeowner. *Minuses:* Few minuses discovered; quality soaker hoses made from rubber or vinyl are more expensive than others, but last longer.

recommendation holds true for both garden beds and container plants. The reason for such thorough and deep watering is to encourage deep-rooted plants. Superficial watering encourages shallow-rooted, less vigorous plants that cannot tap reserves of water deeper in the soil. Consequently, the plant may die during even brief periods of drought or high summer temperatures.

Is your garden getting enough water? You can check by investing in a reliable rain gauge to keep track of the amount of moisture in the garden. Also, feel the soil to see if it needs watering. Dry soil feels warm; moist soil is cool. When garden soil has been improved, as described in this book, it's easy to probe beneath the surface to see how deep the moisture level is. Garden centers sell inexpensive soil moisture meters that help you read soil moisture.

How often should you water? That can be a vexing question because water needs depend on a number of variables, including the type of plant, soil type and slope, temperature, humidity,

specific site (sun or shade), and wind conditions. Soils should also be allowed to dry out slightly between waterings.

It's far better and far more conservative to check the moisture level of the soil and water when needed than to routinely follow a time schedule. The amount of water is more important than the timing of the application.

If you water with sprinklers, turn them on early in the day. This gives plants a chance to dry out before nightfall. Plants with wet foliage are more easily plagued by fungal diseases, which thrive in moist, dark places.

During hot weather, most garden experts feel that a light shower cools leaf surfaces and prevents plant dehydration.

Watering Equipment

There are many ways to apply water to a garden, and each method has benefits and drawbacks, depending on the region, climate, specific site, soil, and types of plants. For an evaluation of watering systems, see page 73.

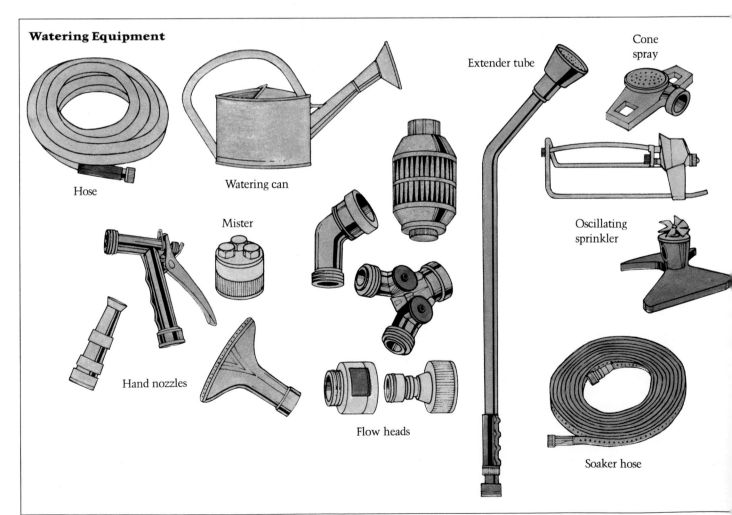

Watering Equipment

Hose

Watering can

Mister

Hand nozzles

Flow heads

Extender tube

Cone spray

Oscillating sprinkler

Soaker hose

Shallow/Deep Watering

Light watering causes shallow roots (left); deep watering forces roots into the soil.

Aptly named, this ooze tube allows water to seep slowly down into the soil, preventing any runoff.

Hoses The simplest equipment for watering, a watering can and garden hose with nozzle or bubbler are suitable for small gardens. Buy the best hose available to avoid the aggravation of hoses that refuse to unkink, break at their connectors, or simply don't last.

Nozzles, bubblers, and hose-end devices called breakers should deliver water gently, not in a hard stream that can injure tender plants and erode soil. A reel or hanger will make it easier to store a garden hose. Other fittings, gadgets, and attachments that make garden hoses more handy include quick-connect devices, double hose shutoffs, gooseneck couplings, hose guides, and hose repair kits.

Designed like a probe, deep-root irrigators attach to a garden hose and efficiently deliver water down to a tree's or large plant's root zone. They can also help aerate compacted or heavy soils and even deliver fertilizer.

Soaker hoses can be an efficient solution to watering. Perforated soakers emit water from a series of holes that can be directed downward for soaking and upward for a fine spray. Another type, a recycled rubber or plastic tube, oozes water along its entire length. Both kinds of soaker hoses can be snaked aboveground throughout the garden or buried under the soil surface to provide a more permanent type of watering system.

Sprinklers These come in many forms, some handier than others. Most common for home use are the oscillating and revolving sprinklers.

Because of their limited range, they are less convenient than a permanent sprinkler system but also much less expensive. Impulse sprinklers, the kind most often used on golf courses and in plant nurseries, are good at delivering water exactly where it's needed, once one has mastered the technique of adjusting the controls.

Underground sprinkler systems are convenient for big gardens with large expanses of lawn. With proper installation, even coverage is achieved with a minimum of guesswork. The system can be set to operate automatically at certain times of day for precise periods of time. Even though the advent of polyvinyl chloride (PVC) pipe made it easier for handy gardeners to install their own sprinkler systems, such installations are best done by professionals.

The flexible drip irrigation system, an aboveground water conservation method, includes lengths of small hoses with numerous small emitters to water each plant or distribute water over a larger area with microsprayers or minisprinklers. It can be a complicated system for large gardens; therefore, it's advisable to start with a small setup.

PLANT CHOICES FOR SPECIAL SOIL CONDITIONS

Improving garden soil increases the odds of growing healthy plants. But even when the soil has been amended, there are situations under which it may be difficult to grow the usual variety of plants. That's why it pays to know how to select species that thrive under adverse conditions. Since healthy plants usually have few problems with pests or disease, this choice is particularly important.

Special plantings can be valuable in areas where water is in short supply because of low rainfall or periods of drought. At the other extreme, consider specially selected plants for sites receiving too much water: low swales with standing water, areas of poor drainage, and soggy sites near lakes, rivers, and other large bodies of water.

Building Soil Basins

Soil basins are circular depressions constructed to direct water to the root zones of trees and large shrubs. They are also useful for watering widely spaced vegetable plantings, such as tomatoes.

Build a shallow watering basin just outside the plant's drip line. Add a second ring about 6 inches away from the plant trunk to keep it dry. As the plant grows, keep moving the basins outside the drip line.

To thoroughly water trees in basically loam soil, fill the basin once, let it drain, and repeat. Trees in clay soil will need the basin filled at least three times; those in sandy soil will require the basin filled only once (if the soil is extremely porous, let the hose run for several minutes to fill).

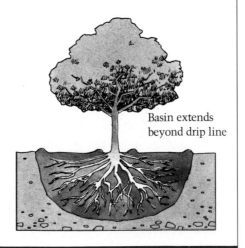

Basin extends beyond drip line

Certain plants grow vigorously in saline soils or near the ocean, even though they may be exposed to salt in the air or through the water. Others relish acid soils, or can withstand buffeting wind.

Where you place a plant also affects its growth. Plants should be carefully selected for their specific site: sunny or shady, on the cold or the warm side of the house.

In all of these special circumstances, soil plays a part. Improving the soil makes the selected plants stronger and better able to cope with stress. Wise choices of plant varieties for specific sites and climates should go hand in hand with improving the garden soil. Good soil broadens the plants' adaptability, making it possible to grow even less-suited varieties in demanding conditions.

Limited-Water Plantings

Drought-tolerant plantings are candidates for gardens with limited water supplies. This xeriscape approach to gardening takes advantage of a plants' genetic ability to use water efficiently. Native plants are good prospects for this type of landscaping.

Xeriscaping is particularly popular in the arid southwestern part of the country and, increasingly, in California, where water rationing limits plant choices. Low-maintenance gardens in areas with hot, dry summers also are likely prospects.

Honeylocust (*Gleditsia triacanthos*) and the junipers (*Juniperus* species) are among the woody plants that can thrive with limited water. Yuccas and cacti are plant groups with a number of choices for desert gardening. Perennial plants native to the American prairies and plains, such as butterfly flower (*Asclepias tuberosa*), goldenrod (*Solidago* species), and purple coneflower (*Echinacea purpurea*), are top choices for dry gardens. Ornamental grasses and sedums include varieties that can get by on comparatively little moisture. Many of the more commonly grown herbs, including sage, lavender, rosemary, and thyme, can tolerate fairly dry conditions. Zinnias and gazanias are good annual choices for dry, sunny gardens.

Plants for Soggy Sites

If natural drainage is poor or a garden site is located near water, choosing plants that can cope with wet soils may be far easier than trying

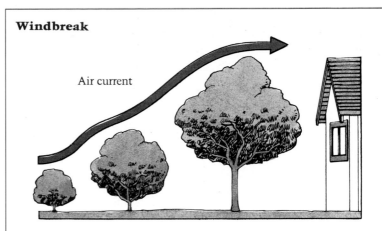

Windbreak

Air current

Proper plant choices can direct breezes and lessen the drying effect of the wind on the soil

to correct the drainage problem. This site might even offer the opportunity to construct an attractive water garden.

For soggy or boggy gardens, alders (*Alnus* species), willows (*Salix* species), and tamarack (*Larix laricina*) are trees of choice. Shrubs well adapted to soggy soils include bog-rosemary (*Andromeda polifolia*), dogwoods (*Cornus* species), and Canada yew (*Taxus canadensis*). Perennial choices might be many of the irises and daylilies (*Hemerocallis*) as well as great lobelia (*Lobelia siphilitica*). Impatiens (*Impatiens wallerana*) is one annual that will tolerate damp ground.

Plants for Oceanside Gardens

For gardens where salt is a problem, either in the soil or because of nearby salty water, it may not be possible to protect the plants completely from this exposure. But, fortunately, some plants are surprisingly tolerant of saline conditions.

Good trees for salt-exposed gardens are white poplar (*Populus alba*), Monterey cypress (*Cupressus macrocarpa*), and holly oak (*Quercus ilex*). Euonymus, which comes in a number of bushy varieties, saltspray rose (*Rosa rugosa*), and thorny elaeagnus (*Elaeagnus pungens*) are among the shrub choices. For

perennials, try sea thrift (*Armeria* species), red-hot-poker (*Kniphofia uvaria*), and lyme-grass (*Elymus arenarius*).

Plants for Windy Garden Sites

Some garden locations are plagued with wind, either from direct blasts or from air being funneled between buildings. Constant buffeting can be tough on plants; strong winds can knock down all but the ground-hugging garden dwarfs. Even constant breezes cause plants to dry out. The following plantings cope best with wind conditions.

Mountain ash (*Sorbus aucuparia*), Norway spruce (*Picea abies*), and plane tree maple (*Acer pseudoplatanus*) stand up well in wind. Such shrubs as rose-of-Sharon (*Hypericum calycinum*), shrubby cinquefoil (*Potentilla fruticosa*), and common snowberry (*Symphoricarpos albus*) are also wind tolerant. Perennials for a windy garden include 'Coronation Gold' yarrow (*Achillea filipendulina*), Japanese anemone (*Anemone japonica*), and maidenhairgrasses (*Miscanthus* species). For annuals, try hawksbeard (*Crepis rubra*), and the annual quaking grasses (*Briza* species).

Plants for Acid Soils

The northeastern and northwestern parts of the United States are likely to have acid soil and high average rainfall, ideal conditions for those comparatively few plants that prefer them. In such areas, it's far simpler to grow acid-loving plants than to continually correct the soil.

Azaleas and rhododendrons require acid soil, a constant supply of moisture, and good drainage.

Good trees for acid soil include dogwood (*Cornus kousa*), red maple (*Acer rubrum*), and sweet gum (*Liquidamber styraciflua*). Heather (*Calluna vulgaris*), highbush blueberry (*Vaccinium corymbosum*), and azaleas and rhododendrons (*Rhododendron* species) are shrubs well adapted to acidity. Hardy perennials might include bishop's-hat (*Epimedium* × *rubrum*), many true lilies (*Lilium* species), and trilliums (*Trillium* species). Fibrous begonias (*Begonia semperflorens*), annual lupines (*Lupinus* species), and annual gentians (*Gentiana* species) are some handsome seasonal plantings.

Planting for Exposure

Entire books have been written on the plants to choose for sunny and for shady garden sites. The great majority of vegetables as well as ornamental flowering plants thrive in a site that receives at least 6 to 8 hours of sun each day. The choices of flowering plants for shady locations are fewer, but favorite shade plants, such as coleus, ferns, and hostas, with handsome foliage of different colors and textures, make up for their lack of showy blossoms.

Gardens surrounding buildings and other structures have different exposures and often very different microclimates depending on which side they are located. Those on the north will be shadier and cooler because sunlight is limited and weak; those on the south will be

Plant Symptoms Due to Other Than Nutritional Causes

Symptom*	Possible Causes
Wilting foliage	Too little or too much water in plant tissues. Too much water causes breakdown of plant systems. Common in freshly transplanted plants where injured roots can't take up enough water to make up for losses of moisture from foliage through transpiration. Common on hot, dry, windy days.
Green foliage turns pale	Commonly caused by too much sun. Happens to shade-loving plants moved to sunny sites.
Plants become leggy, lanky	Often caused by too much shade. Plants that require sun will get leggy and have elongated growth in shady sites.
Growth dwindles	May be caused by a number of situations, including chronic low water supply or too much water (as in poorly draining soils), too much sun or shade, toxic substances in soil, abuse by pets or people.
Foliage appears burned, scorched, and dry	May happen as a result of hot, dry wind, too much exposure to sun without enough water.

* See also chart of symptoms that occur as a result of nutritional deficiencies, page 13.

sunnier and warmer and, with an enriched soil and sufficient moisture, very hospitable to flowering plants.

Gardens on the southwest side of a structure lie in the warmest location of all. Because of the length and intensity of sunlight they receive and the amount of heat radiating from surrounding objects, only plants well adapted to such conditions will survive.

Such sunny sites can be protected from summer heat by shade trees, either deciduous or evergreen. If deciduous trees are chosen, there will be enough sunlight in early spring to plant bulbs and woodland natives.

Before choosing plants for special exposures such as these, analyze the site to determine exactly how much sun it receives, not only in the summer but the year around. This analysis leads to better plant choices, and, consequently, healthier and more productive gardens.

Problem Plants

When plants fail to thrive, it may be due to a number of conditions. Learning to read plant symptoms through foliage and general growth patterns helps diagnose soil problems. But don't blame the soil for a sickly plant until the situation has been assessed carefully. Perhaps the plant is diseased or plagued with pests—or, possibly, it's just in the wrong spot.

Wrong environment   Plants that don't grow well or those that appear sickly may be in the wrong microenvironment. If a shade-loving variety is planted in full sun, it will wilt and its foliage will look pale or scorched. On the other hand, a sun-loving plant positioned in the shade will slow its growth, get very lanky, and appear to dwindle as time goes by.

Plants that require a lot of water will wilt and often die if planted in an overly dry plot; those that get along on minimum amounts but need good drainage will also wilt and die if planted in wet soil. The symptoms may be similar, but investigation quickly reveals the cause.

Another factor that may cause problems with plants is a radical change in the growing situation. If an established plant growing in filtered shade, such as under a tall deciduous tree, is moved to a spot with either more or less sunlight, it may react unfavorably.

As plants develop and mature, their growth reflects the amounts of sunlight, nutrients,

---

Pests and Diseases

Sometimes out of sight is not out of mind. If the perfectly placed plant in the correctly amended soil develops spotted, curled, or oddly colored foliage, or wilts or dies, the cause may be underground pests or soilborne disease. These frustrating problems can be difficult to diagnose and may require extreme measures to control.

Although fungi and bacteria in the soil account for most diseases, a virus may also be to blame. At the first sign of disease, destroy infected plants and clean your garden tools thoroughly. To prevent such diseases, select resistant plant varieties, remove all garden debris, and keep plant foliage dry, especially at night, since fungi thrive in moist conditions.

Though many "ugly bugs" are beneficial, soil-dwelling pests that attack plants include nematodes, root weevils, cutworms, and various other grubs. Controlling them depends on the pest. Nematodes are best curbed by choosing resistant plant varieties. Rotating crops helps lessen pest damage.

Identifying the problem is the first step in finding solutions to pests and diseases. When all else fails, take a sample of the ailing plant, carefully sealed in a plastic bag or container, to a knowledgeable garden center or plant expert, such as an agricultural extension agent, for advice.

---

moisture, and other variables to which they are accustomed, and a change of scene can cause plant stress. Moving the plant to another environment may make it difficult for the existing foliage to function as required, and the plant may struggle to develop new foliage.

Disease   Sometimes plants get diseases from soilborne organisms. Tomatoes are classic examples. They are highly prone to such diseases as fusarium wilt and verticillium wilt, both of which are soilborne fungi.

These problems can be avoided by choosing disease-resistant varieties. In the case of tomatoes, the variety name may be followed by the letters *VF,* which means that the variety is resistant to the diseases mentioned above.

Tall flowering phlox is susceptible to a fungal disease called powdery mildew, but varieties, such as 'Mt. Fujiyama,' have been developed to overcome it. Plant catalogs, garden centers, and *The Ortho Problem Solver* are good sources for information on disease-resistant varieties.

Allelopathic plants   Some plants deal with unwanted competition from other plants by manufacturing substances that discourage their competitors' growth. This action is called allelopathy and usually involves toxic materials that are either produced by the plant itself or by decomposition of plant residue.

Solving Soil Problems

Gardeners around the country face similar soil problems. This chapter describes these gardening challenges and offers some solutions.

Whether landscaping a new home or dealing with established plantings, gardeners face a variety of challenges. Seldom does a site boast ideal soil. It usually needs improving for one reason or another. Yet spotty plant growth can be caused by so many factors that detective work may be necessary to diagnose the problem and find a solution.

New construction can cause compacted soils or loss of topsoil. When the natural lay of the land has been reshaped by a bulldozer, erosion may occur before plant cover has a chance to grow. Hardpan, a comparatively impervious soil layer beneath the surface, can result from earth-moving techniques or from tilling with power equipment to the same depth over an extended period of time. Older, neglected gardens may suffer from heavy root competition or soils lacking nutrients, proper texture, and structure. No one likes to pull up, cut down, or remove growing plants, yet this is exactly what often must be done with overgrown gardens.

In addition to these man-made problems, a number of natural soil conditions must be corrected if vegetables and ornamentals are to thrive. Clay soils, sandy soils, soils with poor drainage, and thin, shallow soils all call for major improvement. Unless corrected, salty soils can burn, badly injure, or kill vegetables and ornamentals. Oddly enough, the solutions for many soil problems that appear quite dissimilar are essentially alike. After a soil has been tested and the laboratory's recommendations implemented, regular amendments of organic matter will create soil that will grow just about anything well.

After diagnosing and correcting soil problems, make sure that plant choices match existing conditions.

Choosing plants adapted to existing conditions also has a great bearing on the success of a garden. Many of the plants recommended for specific soil conditions are natives; others are well-adapted varieties from other parts of the world. Selecting plants that require little water, a plus in many parts of the country where drought is common, is called xeriscaping; in this case it is picking the right plants for the right location.

The following case histories will help gardeners identify specific difficulties and discover some of the available alternatives.

SURFACE SUBSOIL

Subsoil on the soil surface is an unfortunately all-too-common result of home construction, one that many new homeowners must face along with a season or two of mud or dust. Not only does the subsoil create a mess, it's also next to impossible to grow much in it unless it is improved.

When new subdivisions are developed, it is not uncommon for contractors to bulldoze the entire area, sometimes removing the existing topsoil as well as trees and other plants. In some cases, the topsoil ends up under the subsoil as

Topsoil lost during construction of this house had to be replaced.

the construction equipment backfills around buildings. Even the fill dirt brought from another area may be subsoil.

Changing the grade and general configuration of the land is often the excuse for removing the topsoil. Fortunately, this happens less often with an individual home built to an owner's specification than it does with subdivisions. Anyone planning to build a home should make every effort to have the topsoil saved and then replaced after construction is completed.

When the subsoil ends up on the surface as the result of grading and excavating, even weeds don't grow, and the resulting erosion on the bare soil surface can cause problems. A heavy rain can create gulleys in no time. In addition, subsoil is very low in organic matter, usually so much so that it can be called a mineral soil. It may include mineral salts leached from the soil layer originally above it.

Regardless of which of the following solutions are adapted, the first thing to do in this situation is to test the soil, even though the subsoil may look more like clay or, at the other extreme, more like a sandy beach than garden soil. After testing, you can proceed with one or

Converting Subsoil to Topsoil

Subsoil is often as rich as the overlying topsoil in all mineral nutrients except nitrogen and sometimes phosphorus and potash. It lacks organic material and usually has a poor structure. Given enough time, nature converts it into topsoil, but experiments have shown that the process can be speeded up by man.

The Brooklyn Botanic Garden carried out a subsoil-to-topsoil conversion that may be of interest to home gardeners. The subsoil area (hardpan) to be planted in lawn was first plowed in mid-August. Several loads of well-rotted manure were spread over the plowed ground—about 3 to 4 times as much as would be used for ordinary manuring.

Sand (to ensure soil aeration and good drainage), ground limestone (to correct the pH), and 5-10-5 fertilizer were liberally applied, and the whole area was well worked over with a hoe. After being allowed to settle, the area was graded and seeded with Merion bluegrass. A vigorous lawn became established by June of the following season. Weeds were no more of a problem than in any other lawn of their experience.

The same technique was also successfully employed in the preparation of a vegetable garden site on subsoil.

more of the alternatives below, depending on the size of the project, budget, and availability of materials and labor.

1. Find a supplier of topsoil and order enough to cover the area to a depth of at least 4 inches. It may be necessary to remove the subsoil to keep from raising the grade and causing drainage problems. Some contractors can supply good topsoil and do the entire job of spreading, tilling, grading, and fertilizing. This may be an expensive solution, but there is comfort in the fact that once it's done, planting can begin. Cover the soil with mulch and plants as soon as possible to prevent erosion.

2. Plant a cover crop—a green manure— and then cultivate it into the soil to a depth of at least 6 to 8 inches. It's important to get the soil covered with plant growth as quickly as possible. First, till the soil and level the surface. Plant grasses or legumes, then till the crop into the soil when it grows to 6 to 8 inches tall. Ryegrasses, fescue grasses, sweet clovers, and crown vetch are among the best plants to use as green manures or cover crops to prevent erosion.

3. If the area with surface subsoil is fairly small, purchase potting mix from a nursery and till it into the soil, or add 4 to 6 inches of potting soil on top of the subsoil to make a raised bed. Raised beds can be set off from the rest of the yard or garden by timbers, railroad ties, bricks, stones, or any other appropriate,

often ornamental, material. They also can be merely raised mounds above the original soil surface level.

4. Spread a ½-inch to 3-inch layer of leaf mold, moist peat moss, well-rotted manure, or compost on the subsoil and till it into the soil to a depth of 6 to 8 inches. Repeat this procedure two more times, then mulch the surface and commence planting. In some regions, organic materials may be regularly available as industrial waste products or agricultural crops.

5. Use leaves from deciduous trees as an organic additive to improve the subsoil. Shred the leaves and spread them on the subsoil in a layer 4 to 6 inches deep, then till them into the soil to a depth of 6 to 8 inches. The shredded leaves, like green manure, will decay in the soil. Mulch and plant, tilling two to three amendments of leaves into the soil. It's best to wait a month or so before installing permanent plants. That gives the organic matter time to decay.

NEGLECTED, OVERGROWN PLANTINGS

When buying an old home, gardeners seldom inherit a fine garden or good soil. More often, the yard has been badly neglected. Trees may be unkempt, shrubs overgrown, perennials crowded, and garden beds a mix of ornamentals and weeds. It's often very difficult to know where to start. So much needs attention that only the most obvious chores get done.

Combining pavers with raised beds creates a tidy, easy-to-plant vegetable garden.

When trees, shrubs, and other ornamentals have been neglected for long periods, root competition in the soil may be extreme, making it unlikely that heavy-feeding, demanding plants, such as roses, could be vigorous. If trees are very much overgrown, the yard may be so shady that plant selections are severely limited. Neglected trees also may be full of dead wood and badly need trimming and pruning.

If shrubs have grown wild, they probably are full of dead wood. Neglected flowering shrubs may have extremely limited blooms, no blossoms, or very little foliage. Perennial plants receiving too little attention are likely to be overcrowded and much in need of division or moving to a place with better soil and ample nutrients.

The first thing that must be done in neglected yards and gardens is to assess the plants. Unless the gardener is very knowledgeable, it might be wise to call in a professional arborist or horticulturist to identify and provide a comparative rating for all of the major plants. Experts can make recommendations as to which trees and shrubs should be kept and which are of little value.

Sometimes, the value of a tree or shrub is measured by its rarity or its reputation as a variety that performs well and has few bad habits. Sometimes, value lies in the location and landscape function of the plant. Only when plants are evaluated can an objective plan for renovation be made.

When so many things need doing, not everything can be accomplished in a short time. It may take a year or more to get a poorly maintained yard or garden in shape. The following suggestions cover some of the ways to approach the rejuvenation. As always, one of the first things to do is test the soil. The resulting recommendations will show the way to amend and improve the soil.

1. Contract with a professional arborist for removal of undesirable trees and trimming of the others.

2. Remove undesirable shrubs and prune those worth saving. It's possible to rejuvenate some flowering shrubs by cutting them back to about 1 foot. The rule of thumb for annual pruning is to cut back to the ground one quarter to one third of the older growth.

Corrective surgery may be needed to rid neglected trees of dead wood. This apple tree is being pruned during its dormant season to direct new growth.

Crowded Roots

Tree roots compete with nearby plants for moisture and soil nutrients

After careful assessment, the owner decided that this well-established garden needed only judicious trimming.

Some evergreen shrubs begin to grow from old wood after drastic pruning; others don't. Since it's important to know the difference, it's wise to contact a professional for advice or to do the work.

3. Some overcrowded perennials can be revived by dividing. Prepare a new garden bed, removing all of the weeds and old plants; then till plenty of organic matter into the soil. Also add lime, sulfur, and fertilizers at this time, if needed. After mulching the new bed, moisten the ground well. Then dig up, divide, and replant perennials. This can be done at just about any time of the year, but spring and autumn offer the best conditions in most parts of the country.

4. Refrain from buying new trees and shrubs no matter how great the temptation until the older plantings have been assessed, removed or rejuvenated through pruning, divided, or transplanted. A regular regime of soil improvement should then be inaugurated, including amending with organic matter and fertilizing, if needed.

Even though present plants may need care until they are assessed, gardeners may find it easier to save and revive them rather than to try and get new plants established. This is helpful advice for areas with poor soil.

THIN, SHALLOW SOILS

These soils, common on hilltops, hillsides, and throughout mountainous regions, may be the only thing that lies between the ground surface and subsurface rock layers. Thin soils may also cover the top of an impervious underground soil layer known as hardpan. They may lack subsoil and may themselves be both meager and poor in quality.

Soils are considered very shallow if they extend less than 10 inches deep before hitting an impervious layer that retards root growth. They are considered merely shallow if they are between 10 and 20 inches deep.

Shallow soils occur naturally where bedrock lies near the surface. A hardpan lying within a foot or so of the soil surface can even be caused by man, if the soil is mechanically tilled to exactly the same depth over a period of time. Some surprised homeowners find that their thin soils are the result of an underlying concrete sidewalk, former tennis court, or other buried construction.

Trees and shrubs that grow in shallow soils have less physical support from their root systems. Large plants, especially trees, growing in shallow soils are consequently vulnerable to wind injury and frequently blow down.

Gardeners have several alternatives when dealing with shallow soils in a garden.

1. If shallow soil is due to hardpan, it may be necessary to break up only this impervious layer by drilling a few holes to allow proper soil drainage and plant root penetration. Holes should be made every 4 to 6 feet for best results. Severe cases may call for wielding a pick-ax or jackhammer.

2. Another way to deal with the drainage problems caused by hardpan is to construct drains or install drainpipes on top of the hardpan layer to carry water away from the garden area. The exact lay of the land will determine whether or not this is feasible.

3. Raised beds are an attractive and comparatively easy way to deal with both hardpan and other shallow soils. Raised beds can be as simple as an area of well-prepared garden soil heaped 4 to 6 inches higher than the original surface, or as elegant as an area of the garden contained within attractive stone walls.

4. Another way to deal with thin soils is to seek those plants known to have shallow root systems. The list below includes some good choices.

STEEP HILLSIDES

Slopes that are steep are a challenge for most gardeners. They are often difficult to amend, plant, water, and fertilize, and are likely to erode. By their grade, these slopes can also create other problems, such as low fertility, lack of soil moisture, shallow soils, and erosion.

Creative ways to handle steep or hilly gardens center around construction and earth-moving solutions. Terracing, adding permanent containers, carving out plant niches, and using some specially adapted plantings are valuable alternatives.

1. Terraces are good solutions for breaking up the downward plunge of a steep slope. Select

Shallow-rooted plants were used as bright foils for the handsome rock terraces on this hillside.

Shallow-Rooted Plants

Botanical Name	Common Name
Acacia	Acacia
Acer saccharinum	Silver maple
Ailanthus altissima	Tree-of-heaven
Alnus	Alder
Eucalyptus	Eucalyptus
Ficus	Fig
Fraxinus uhdei	Evergreen ash
Gleditsia	Honeylocust
Morus	Mulberry
Platanus	Plane tree, sycamore
Populus	Poplar
Rhus	Sumac
Robinia	Black locust
Salix	Willow
Ulmus	Elm

timbers, stones, or any sturdy material that makes a good retaining wall and can be moored securely on the hillside.

2. Plants can be grown in containers installed permanently on the slope.

3. Small individual planting holes can be scooped out of the slope and treated almost as a planting container. Small basins are created in the sloping soil, given lips to hold water and planting material, and then planted with small to medium-sized ornamentals or vegetables.

4. A combination of alpines, rock garden inhabitants, smaller ground-hugging plants, and creeping vines would be good choices for hillside gardens.

ACID SOILS

These soils are common in areas of heavy rainfall, including the northeastern and northwestern parts of the United States. Acid soils can be sandy, loaded with clay, or have too much peat moss. When sedges, mosses, and grasses decay in wet conditions, acid soil with a high percentage of organic matter is the result.

First of all, get a soil test to determine the pH level. The lab will tell you exactly how acid the soil is and give recommendations for correcting this and any other soil problems.

The difficulty with acid soil is that many of the nutrients needed for plant growth become less available because they are converted into

Top: Making use of every inch of the hillside, innovative gardeners added raised beds to grow crops and ornamentals.
Bottom: Embellished with shrubs and flowers, stone steps allow easy access to a steep slope.

*Top: Bunchberry,
a small perennial,
related to the dogwood
family, prefers acid
soil with generous
amounts of humus.
Bottom: Lime and
bonemeal amendments
are worked into this
acid soil before
planting.*

Plants for *Acid Soils*

Botanical Name	Common Name
Trees and Shrubs	
Amelanchier	Serviceberry
Arctostaphylos	Manzanita
Calluna	Heather
Camellia	Camellia
Cytisus	Broom
Erica	Heath
Gardenia	Gardenia
Hydrangea	Hydrangea
Ilex	Holly
Kalmia latifolia	Mountain laurel
Lagerstroemia indica	Crapemyrtle
Leucothoe	Leucothoe
Magnolia	Magnolia
Picea	Spruce
Pieris	Andromeda
Pinus	Pine
Populus tremuloides	Quaking aspen
Quercus palustris	Pin oak
Rhododendron	Rhododendron, azalea
Salix babylonica	Weeping willow
Sorbus	Mountain ash
Tsuga	Hemlock
Flowers	
Convallaria	Lily-of-the-valley
Coreopsis	Coreopsis
Gypsophila	Baby's breath
Lupinus	Lupine

insoluble salts. Other elements such as aluminum and manganese can become water soluble, often in amounts that are toxic to plants. The microorganism activity that causes decay is less in acid soils; therefore, organic matter will not break down as fast.

There are normally two main ways to deal with acid soil. The first is to treat the soil chemically; the second is to grow plants that normally grow best in acid soils. Acid-loving plants, including those listed on the previous page, thrive in soils with a low pH.

1. Treating the soil chemically to raise the pH is done by adding garden lime. Dolomitic garden lime is recommended because it contains both calcium and magnesium, nutrients

Raising pH With Limestone

The following chart shows the number of pounds of ground limestone (calcium carbonate) needed per 100 square feet to raise soil pH to 6.5. If the change is to be drastic and the recommended amounts of limestone are large, the limestone should be added in several stages. Dolomitic limestone is recommended because it adds magnesium as well as calcium to the soil. The limestone should be cultivated into the soil.

	Pounds of Limestone Per 100 Square Feet		
Current pH	**Sandy Loam**	**Loam**	**Clay Loam**
4.0	11.5	16	23
4.5	9.5	13.5	19.5
5.0	8	10.5	15
5.5	6	8	10.5
6.0	3	4	5.5

Fast-growing Salix babylonica *(weeping willow) needs plenty of water and even tolerates poor drainage.*

usually deficient in acid soils. Follow the recommendations of the soil laboratory and beware of adding too much lime.

The chart on page 89 shows how much ground limestone is required to raise the pH level of 100 square feet of soil.

2. The other way to solve this soil problem is to use plants that adapt well to acid soils. Some of the plantings that will grow well in soils with pH levels of 4.5 to 5.5 are listed on page 88.

WET SOILS

Many plants are ill-suited for growing in wet and waterlogged soils. The reason is that when the spaces between soil particles become filled with water, they lack enough air for most root systems to survive, and the plant drowns. Fortunately, some plants have evolved over the years to cope with conditions presented by soggy soils.

Wet soils result from a number of natural and man-made conditions. An area may have a high water table or natural springs, with resident water so near the soil surface that the ground is always wet and perhaps even boggy in character. Other causes may be hardpan or thin soil (described on page 85), blocked or broken storm sewers, and leaking ponds.

In neighborhoods where new construction is underway, wet soils may be caused by changing grades and adding structures that create new runoff paths for rain. Even gentle slopes allow water to course through areas between buildings like raging rivers, and settle in low swales, where soils soon become waterlogged and water stands on the surface.

If wet soils occur only once in a while and then only after unusually heavy rains, the condition probably isn't serious. But if the soil in an area remains wet even during drier seasons, a solution may be desired or even necessary.

Some alternatives for wet soils are fairly simple and inexpensive; others may require engineering skills and a fairly large budget.

1. Drying out large gardens with severe drainage problems calls for expert assistance for everything from design to laying drainpipe. A top-quality drainage system is not a job for an amateur gardener unless that amateur is also a civil engineer. Fortunately, most drainage problems are not that serious.

2. Smaller gardens with wet soil problems are easier to improve. If better drainage is the aim, raised beds can be a simple alternative and one that allows the usual assortment of ornamental plants to literally rise above the problem.

3. A system of trenching with drainage pipes or French drains (shallow trenches with gravel covered by soil) often adequately improves the drainage of a small garden bed.

Left: Colorful primulas make hardy growers in cool, moist climates. Some varieties are native bog dwellers. Right: A maple tree's canopy of leaves requires a constant supply of water, making it a good choice for marshy gardens.

4. Lawns with low areas that become soggy at the first hint of rain often can be drained by spiking a network of holes through the turf with tines of a garden fork. Because wet soils are far more susceptible to compaction than dry soils, the area may have been damaged by people walking on it.

5. One obvious yet often overlooked solution to wet soils is to create a water garden or bog garden in the damp area. Another good solution is to select plants that are genetically programmed to thrive in unusual soil conditions. Some plants that grow well in wet soil are shown in the chart below.

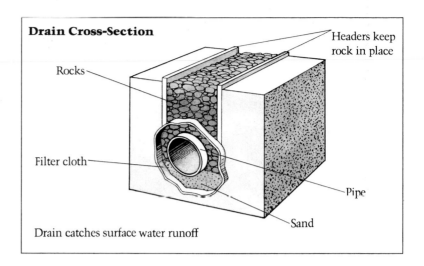

Drain Cross-Section

Headers keep rock in place
Rocks
Filter cloth
Pipe
Sand

Drain catches surface water runoff

Plants for Wet Soils

Botanical Name	Common Name	Botanical Name	Common Name
Trees		**Perennials**	
Acer rubrum	Red maple	*Aconitum*	Monkshood
A. saccharinum	Silver maple	*Acorus calamus*	Sweet flag
Alnus	Alder	*Althea officinalis*	Marshmallow
Amelanchier arborea	Serviceberry	*Aster novae-angliae*	New England aster
Betula nigra	River birch	*Astilbe*	Astilbe
Casuarina equisetifolia	Horsetail tree	*Caltha palustris*	Marshmarigold
Ilex cassine	Dahoon holly	*Cimicifuga racemosa*	Black snakeroot
I. opaca	American holly	*Colocasia esculenta*	Elephant's-ear
Larix laricina	American larch	*Cyperus*	Sedge
Liquidamber styraciflua	Sweet gum	*Eupatorium maculatum*	Joe-pye-weed
Magnolia virginiana	Sweet bay	*Hydrophyllum*	Virginia waterleaf
Nyssa sylvatica	Sourgum	*virginianum*	
Platanus	Plane tree, sycamore	*Iris kaempferi*	Japanese iris
Populus	Poplar	*I. sibirica*	Siberian iris
Quercus bicolor	Swamp white oak	*Lilium canadense*	Canada lily
Q. palustris	Pin oak	*Lobelia cardinalis*	Cardinal flower
Salix	Willow	*L. siphilitica*	Great lobelia
Taxodium distichum	Bald cypress	*Lysimachia nummularia*	Moneywort
Tristania laurina	Brisbane box	*Mentha*	Mint
		Myosotis scorpioides	Forget-me-not
Shrubs		*Phalaris arundinacea*	Ribbongrass
Aronia arbutifolia	Red chokeberry	var. *picta*	
Bambusa disticha	Fernleaf bamboo	*Polypodiaceae*	Fern family
Betula occidentalis	Water birch	*Primula japonica*	Japanese primrose
Calycanthus	Sweetshrub	*Ranunculus*	Buttercup
Cephalanthus occidentalis	Buttonbush	*Sanguinaria canadensis*	Bloodroot
Cornus sericea	Redosier dogwood	*Sisyrinchium*	Golden-eyed grass
Ilex glabra	Gallberry	*californicum*	
I. verticillata	Winterberry	*Tolmiea menziesii*	Piggyback plant
Lindera benzoin	Spicebush	*Trollius*	Globe flower
Myrica pensylvanica	Bayberry	*Typha latifolia*	Common cattail
Rhododendron	Smooth azalea	*Viola blanda*	Sweet white violet
arborescens		*V. lanceolata*	Lance-leafed violet
R. vaseyi	Pink-shell azalea	*Zantedeschia*	Calla lily
Rosa palustris	Swamprose		
Salix	Willow		
Thuja	Arborvitae		
Viburnum trilobum	Cranberrybush		

Corn grows well in the clay soil of the Navajo and Hopi Indian reservations.

Working Clay Soil

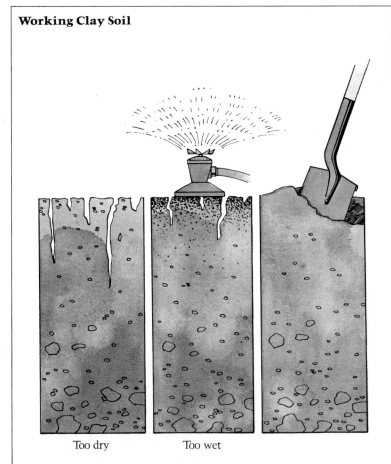

Too dry   Too wet

Heavy clay soil is hard to work when too dry or wet. For easiest tilling, simply moisten ahead of time.

HEAVY SOILS

These soils, which have a high proportion of clay, are difficult to work and can be extremely hard to till. When clay soils are too wet, they're sticky and compact easily; if too dry, tilling them is like tilling pottery. When overwatered, heavy soils may contain little air. Soil pores may be too small and too few.

Adding organic matter is the major key to improving the texture and structure of these heavy soils. A layer of organic matter 1 to 4 inches thick should be spread on the soil surface and tilled into the soil to a depth of 6 to 8 inches or more each time the soil is worked. Use well-rotted manure, compost, leaf mold, or other organic material available locally, such as grape pomace, cottonseed, and sawdust.

When heavy, clay soils are well managed through the addition of organic matter, they develop a structure that holds both water and nutrients well. This type of soil needs less fertilizer and less supplemental watering than other soils.

Soil tests can be a help in managing heavy soils that may be either acid or alkaline. Once the test results and recommendations have come back from the laboratory, a plan for improving the soil can be implemented.

A number of solutions are possible for dealing with this kind of soil. Often several ideas

When tilled into heavy soil, well-rotted leaf mold will improve soil texture and structure.

Double-Digging

Starting at one end of the row, remove a spadeful of soil and place at the other end (1). Work soil amendment into the lower level of exposed soil (2). Then dig another trench (3), filling in the first with a mixture of soil and amendment. Continue to the end of the bed.

can be used in different parts of the garden, depending on the size of the garden bed, the exposure, and other environmental factors.

1. If it's possible for the area to remain out of production for a season or two, plant a green manure crop and till it into the soil. Then let the soil sit for several weeks to let the green manure decompose. While it's idle, cover with hay, straw, or another type of mulch to prevent erosion.

2. For the first two to three years of working heavy soil, plant only annual vegetables or ornamentals. That way it's easy to work 1 to 4 inches of organic matter, compost, peat moss, or manure into the top foot or more of the heavy, clay soil.

3. Use the old-fashioned method of double-digging to work layers of organic matter into the soil. Double-digging ensures that both the subsoil and topsoil are improved to the depth of two spade blades.

4. If the garden area is just too large to improve easily, use raised beds and containers with artificial or imported soils for gardening. A mix of one part existing soil plus one part imported or artificial soil should make a good planting medium.

SANDY SOILS

These soils, with as much as 85 to 90 percent sand particles, are difficult to manage. They don't hold water well and they are not very

Ornamental crab apples aren't too fussy, but they grow best in well-drained soil.

fertile. Excessively sandy soils are characteristically gritty to the touch. Their large pores make it just as easy for water to run out as in. Nutrients also slip in and out of sandy soils just as easily.

On the plus side, these soils are not prone to erosion by water, since the water goes right through them. But they can be easily eroded by wind, depending on the specific location and prevailing winds. Sandy soils are easy to cultivate. They don't get too wet and they don't get sticky like heavy, clay soils.

Adding organic matter or clay and organic matter to sandy soils is the only way to increase their ability to retain water and nutrients. Compost, peat moss, well-rotted manure, or other easily available organic matter would be good choices for working into sandy soils. If soils are not improved in this manner, plant maintenance must include frequent watering and frequent light fertilizing with slow-release fertilizers.

The following methods are the most successful ways to deal with sandy soil problems.

Top: A seacoast favorite, brilliant ice plants such as this Lampranthus *flourish in sandy soil. Bottom: Attractive as a border planting, variegated liriope needs good drainage.*

Ratio of Amendment to Soil

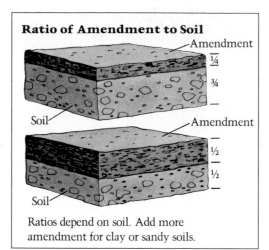

Ratios depend on soil. Add more amendment for clay or sandy soils.

1. Several times a year, work a thick layer of organic matter, as much as 4 to 6 inches, into the top 8 to 12 inches of soil, using a recommended material such as compost, peat moss, or manure. For the first couple of years, it would be easiest to grow only annual vegetables and ornamentals so that the soil can be easily tilled and improved.

2. Raised beds may be a logical answer if a gardener wants to grow plants such as peonies that thrive on rich, highly organic soils.

3. The easiest solution of all is simply to grow plants that like sandy soils. There are many selections for almost all gardens.

Plants for Sandy Soils

Botanical Name	Common Name	Botanical Name	Common Name
Trees		*Lonicera tatarica*	Tatarian honeysuckle
Crataegus phaenopyrum	Washington hawthorn	*Myrica cerifera*	Wax myrtle
Elaeagnus angustifolia	Russian olive	*M. pensylvanica*	Bayberry
Ilex opaca	American holly	*Philadelphus coronarius*	Mock orange
Juniperus virginiana	Eastern red cedar	*Potentilla fruticosa*	Shrubby cinquefoil
Malus	Crab apple	*Prunus maritima*	Beach plum
Nyssa sylvatica	Sourgum	*Pyracantha coccinea*	Firethorn
Parkinsonia aculeata	Jerusalem thorn	*Rhamnus cathartica*	Common buckthorn
Picea glauca	White spruce	*Rhus glabra*	Smooth sumac
Pinus banksiana	Jack pine	*Rosa rugosa*	Japanese rose
P. echinata	Yellow pine	*Spiraea japonica*	Japanese spiraea
P. elliottii	Slash pine	*Tamarix parviflora*	Tamarisk
P. resinosa	Red pine	*Vaccinium corymbosum*	Highbush blueberry
P. rigida	Pitch pine	*Weigela florida*	Weigela
P. strobus	Eastern white pine		
P. thunbergiana	Japanese black pine	**Vines and Ground Covers**	
P. virginiana	Scrub pine	*Actinidia arguta*	Hardy kiwi
Platanus × *acerifolia*	London plane tree	*Arctostaphylos uva-ursi*	Manzanita
Populus alba	White poplar	*Campsis radicans*	Trumpet creeper
Quercus alba	White oak	*Celastrus scandens*	American bittersweet
Q. palustris	Pin oak		
Q. stellata	Post oak	*Juniperus chinensis* var. *procumbens*	Japanese garden juniper
Sophora japonica	Japanese pagoda tree	*J. conferta*	Shore juniper
		J. horizontalis	Creeping juniper
Shrubs		*Lantana montevidensis*	Trailing lantana
Aronia arbutifolia	Red chokeberry	*Liriope spicata*	Lilyturf
Berberis thunbergii	Japanese barberry	*Lonicera japonica* 'Halliana'	Hall's Japanese honeysuckle
Buddleia davidii	Orange-eye butterflybush	*Parthenocissus quinquefolia*	Virginia creeper
Chaenomeles speciosa	Flowering quince		
Juniperus chinensis 'Pfitzerana'	Pfitzer juniper	*Phyla nodiflora*	Lippia
		Pteridium aquilinum	Bracken
Kalmia angustifolia	Sheep laurel	*Rhus aromatica*	Fragrant sumac
K. latifolia	Mountain laurel	*Rosa wichuraiana*	Memorial rose
Kerria japonica	Japanese rose	*Sedum acre*	Golden carpet
Lespedeza thunbergii	Bushclover	*Thymus vulgaris*	Common thyme
Ligustrum amurense	Amur privet	*Vitis*	Grape
		Wedelia trilobata	Wedelia

Top: This south-western garden reflects its surroundings, making extensive use of native plants. Bottom: Xeriscaped with cacti and other arid-climate plantings, this landscape is drought tolerant.

ARID SOUTHWEST AND ALKALINE SOILS

Although most plants grow well in slightly basic soils, with a pH level slightly above the neutral point of 7.0, there are some that will grow in a soil that is very basic, or sweet, with a pH of 7.5 or above. At higher pH levels (8.0 or more), such plant nutrients as iron and manganese become unavailable to plants because they are transformed into insoluble salts.

In areas where the rainfall averages less than 20 inches per year, it's likely that the soil is alkaline. A good example is the American Southwest. Although irrigation can solve problems of too little water and too much alkalinity, it's an expensive solution for most areas, both from an economical and an environmental point of view.

Plants growing in soil that is too basic may develop easy-to-recognize symptoms that indicate nutrient shortages due to high soil alkalinity: for instance, leaves may become chlorotic—the veins stay green but the tissue between the veins turn yellow because the plant is unable to get iron. Changing the soil pH makes those nutrients once again available to plants.

As with acid soils, there are two main ways to deal with the problem once a soil test reveals that indeed the ground is alkaline. Chemicals can be added to lower the pH, or plants can be selected that will grow well in this type of soil.

This high-desert garden requires no maintenance. The plantings help divert wind and control damaging erosion.

Plants for Alkaline Soils

Botanical Name	Common Name
Trees and Shrubs	
Acer negundo	Boxelder
Albizia julibrissin	Silk tree
Berberis thunbergii	Japanese barberry
Casuarina	Beefwood
Celtis	Hackberry
Cercocarpus	Mountain mahogany
Deutzia	Deutzia
Elaeagnus angustifolia	Russian olive
Forsythia × intermedia	Forsythia
Fraxinus velutina	Velvet ash
Hibiscus syriacus	Rose-of-Sharon
Kerria japonica	Japanese rose
Lonicera fragrantissima	Fragrant honeysuckle
Malus sargentii	Sargent crab apple
Philadelphus	Mock orange
Phoenix dactylifera	Date palm
Populus fremontii	Fremont cottonwood
Potentilla fruticosa	Bush cinquefoil
Robinia	Locust
Sophora japonica	Japanese pagoda tree
Spiraea × vanhouttei	Bridalwreath
Viburnum dentatum	Arrowwood
V. dilatatum	Linden viburnum
Washingtonia	Washington palm
Zizyphus jujuba	Common jujube

1. To correct a high pH in garden soils, apply aluminum sulfate, ferrous sulfate, or soil sulfur at the rate of 2 pounds per 100 square feet. Wait a couple of weeks and then repeat the soil test for pH. Continue with this two-step process until the soil pH is at the desired level for the plants you wish to grow.

2. An easier solution is to choose plants, many of them natives, that thrive in dry, alkaline soils. Called xeriscaping, this type of gardening includes choosing plants that thrive on very little water. It's an environmentally sound and conservative way to landscape. Many American natives are well-equipped to deal with low annual rainfall, and offer attractive alternatives to moisture-loving plantings. The list at left gives an idea of the type of plants that grow in alkaline soils with pH levels of 7.5 to 8.4.

ERODED SOILS

Both water and wind can erode soils. Water erosion happens most often when the ground is unplanted, bare, and unprotected from the elements by plant roots and foliage. Erosion by wind occurs mainly in areas with uncommonly high prevailing gusts, such as on mountain tops, over flat prairies, and along the ocean. Water usually creates the most damage in the shortest time.

The steeper the slope, the more likely the chance of erosion. It can be caused by rain transforming bare soil into flowing rivers of mud or by surface water carrying soil particles downhill. As the soil erodes, gullies and channels develop and deepen.

The keys to halting erosion are to cover the soil and to reduce or break up the steep plane of the slope. Dense plantings of low plants slow and even stop erosion on slight slopes. A heavy mulch combined with a thick ground cover will help hold the soil in place. Once the plants grow, both their roots and their foliage diminish the destructive effect of falling rain and flowing water. Several attractive and effective solutions for preventing soil erosion are outlined below.

1. Plant ryegrass or another quick-growing ground cover as a temporary nurse crop to hold the soil while desirable plants are getting established. Before planting on steep slopes, first cover the soil with a coarse netting sold for this purpose. Keep the ground moist until the seedlings are well established.

Once the ground is stabilized, other plants can be put into the soil. Mulch the soil as the plantings are made. The original nurse crop can be covered with mulch or cut and tilled into the soil as other plants take hold.

2. Diminish slope by terracing the ground with a series of ornamental retaining walls and raised beds. This type of design discourages the free flow of water by cutting out its former pathways.

3. Use ornamental plantings to divert both wind and water. Install the plants in such a way that they cut up and slow down the flow of water during rainstorms. Carefully planted screens such as trees and shrubs, placed on the side of the property from which the prevailing winds blow, will help keep soil in place by directing the wind upward. Choose fast growers, and avoid plants with brittle branches that can be snapped off easily by gusts of wind.

COMPACTED SOILS

Like hardpan and shallow soils, compacted soil creates problems in the garden because water and nutrients do not flow freely through the soil. Water stands on the surface because it can't soak into the hard ground.

Compacted soil is caused by repeated traffic, either foot or vehicular. The weight of the

Beachside plantings of grasses and conifers tie down sand and slow the erosion of the slope.

constant traffic breaks down the soil structure, packing it so that the soil pores are deprived of their full complement of air. When this happens, plant roots have a hard time penetrating the soil. Sandy soils are least likely to become compacted; heavy and loamy soils are the most susceptible. Wet soils compact far easier than dry soils.

There are two main ways to deal with this problem. The first is to divert traffic from easily compacted areas with pathways and plantings; the second is to correct the compaction.

1. Compacted soil often occurs along a regular traffic route, an area of easy access. If this area lies in the pathway of traffic, the best approach is to construct a regular path with stepping-stones, pavers, or some other ornamental surface.

2. Prevent compaction from taking place by altering the traffic through an area. This can

Top: Carefully placed to divert traffic, this ornamental border keeps visitors on the walkway and off the lawn.
Bottom: To avoid compacting the soil, boards are laid on the surface.

be difficult if the property represents a known shortcut to schools or other popular destinations. Change traffic patterns with fences or plants. Prickly plants are strong deterrents to both people and animals.

3. Correct the soil in compacted areas by first aerating and then tilling it. A large area may require a mechanical tiller. At this time, make regular amendments of organic matter and other soil amendments if soil tests have indicated low levels of nutrients or the wrong pH level.

SALINE SOILS

Salty soils are found in a number of different regions, particularly those in arid and semiarid climates without enough rainfall to leach the salts through the soil. In most desert areas, irrigation water itself may be high in salts.

Saline soils are also common near the ocean where strong onshore winds carry salty spray inland and deposit it on gardens, where it creates problems for plant roots and foliage. Salt spray on plant foliage makes leaves look as though they're scorched or burned. In extreme cases, it can even kill the plant. In diagnosing the problems of ailing plants in these areas, it's always wise to think about the possibilities of salt contamination.

Soils adjacent to walkways and roadways that are salted in winter to prevent icing often receive enough salts to damage plants. Storm drainage systems can carry this salty water into gardens a considerable distance from the original site.

Soluble salts in the soil that cause trouble for gardeners include common table salt as well as salts of potassium, magnesium, and calcium. Those soil salts are the product of the weathering of soil minerals as well as the residue left on soil surfaces when water evaporates. Water can carry dissolved salts from subsoils as it moves upward through the soil. Salts not carried away by rain or irrigation can cause serious plant damage.

Saline soils also include sodic soil, an extremely alkaline soil with a high concentration of free sodium. Sodium ruins soil structure and makes the soil impermeable to water. It may form caustic soda (sodium hydroxide), which dissolves organic matter. One indication of sodic soils is a crusty black surface.

Water is one of the management tools for saline soils, so gardening in areas with low average rainfall can be a challenge.

1. In arid regions of the United States, such as the Southwest, which is noted for salty alkaline soils, gardening is far easier if plant choices are limited to natives. It's usually too difficult to correct and maintain large areas of saline soils because of the amount of water required to leach salts from the soil. Any plants not constituted to tolerate salt should be grown in raised beds or containers with prepared or commercial soil mixes.

The furrow system of growing vegetables in desert saline soils is illustrated on page 102. It could also work for other garden plants. The proximity of the crops to the furrow carrying the irrigation water that leaches the salts away from their roots determines the success or failure of such planting. The best possible location is where the water will move through the plant root zone, carrying the excess salts beyond it.

Water in a furrow will move radially downward through the soil at each side of the furrow, carrying salts with it to the center of the bed if enough water is applied. Planting near the edge of the bed will avoid injury from salt accumulation. Do not plant on the crown or high point of a furrow.

2. Oceanside gardens can be somewhat protected from salt spray borne onshore by wind by placing them on the inland side of sheltering structures. Fences and wind screens also provide some protection from salt-laden breezes. Once again, the choice of salt-tolerant plants makes gardening far easier.

3. Plants in the path of runoff from areas treated with salt during the winter often have their roots in salt-affected soils at the same time that their foliage is being sprayed with salty water from passing vehicles. Where possible, plant leaves should be washed off and salty water leached from root areas by heavy applications of water.

A vine with vibrant blossoms, bougainvillea is tolerant of saline soil but needs protection from frosts.

Salt-Tolerant Plants

Botanical Name	Common Name
Araucaria heterophylla	Norfolk Island pine
Arctotheca calendula	Capeweed
Baccharis pilularis	Coyotebrush
Bougainvillea	Bougainvillea
Callistemon viminalis	Weeping bottlebrush
Carissa grandiflora	Natal plum
Chamaerops humilis	European fan palm
Coprosma repens	Mirrorplant
Cordyline indivisa	Blue dracaena
Cortaderia selloana	Pampasgrass
Delosperma 'Alba'	White ice plant
Drosanthemum	Rosea ice plant
Euonymus japonica	Spindle tree
Gazania	Gazania
Lampranthus spectabilis	Trailing ice plant
Nerium oleander	Oleander
Phyla nodiflora	Lippia
Pinus halepensis	Aleppo pine
Pittosporum crassifolium	Karo
Pyracantha	Firethorn
Rosmarinus officinalis	Rosemary
Syzygium paniculatum	Brush-cherry

Another solution around your own home is to substitute cat litter, ashes, or sand for salt treatment for ice and snow. Use salt-tolerant plants in areas prone to salty runoff.

4. Sodic soils with high percentages of free sodium can be treated with applications of 5 pounds of gypsum (calcium sulfate) for every 100 square feet of soil. The aim is to replace the sodium with calcium.

Till the gypsum into the soil and then water well to leach out the sodium. If this improves the drainage and structure of the soil, the treatment can be repeated with subsequent additions of gypsum.

5. Another choice for gardeners in arid areas with salty soils is to create a desert garden, using rocks, cacti, and other native plants as design features. This drought-tolerant type of gardening is gaining in popularity as gardeners discover its advantages. These attractive gardens are similar in spirit to the lean, spare landscapes of Japan.

6. In cases where salty soils are not too extreme, choosing plants with a high tolerance for saline conditions is the easiest solution. The plants at left make good choices.

Vegetable Beds for Saline Soils

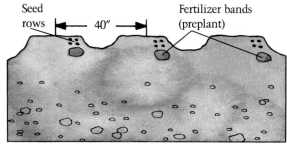

For peppers, chile, okra, eggplant, broccoli, cauliflower, sweet potatoes, cowpeas, summer squash, and sweet corn

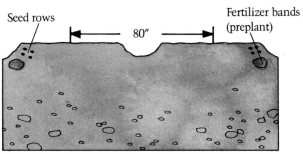

For tomatoes, canteloupe, watermelon, pumpkins, and winter squash

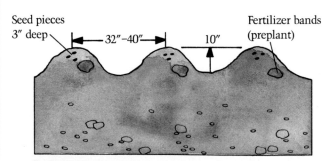

For potatoes

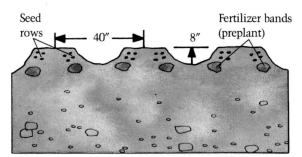

For lettuce, spinach, Swiss chard, cabbage, brussels sprouts, kohlrabi, beets, carrots, turnips, radishes, onions, peas, and beans

U. S. Rainfall Map

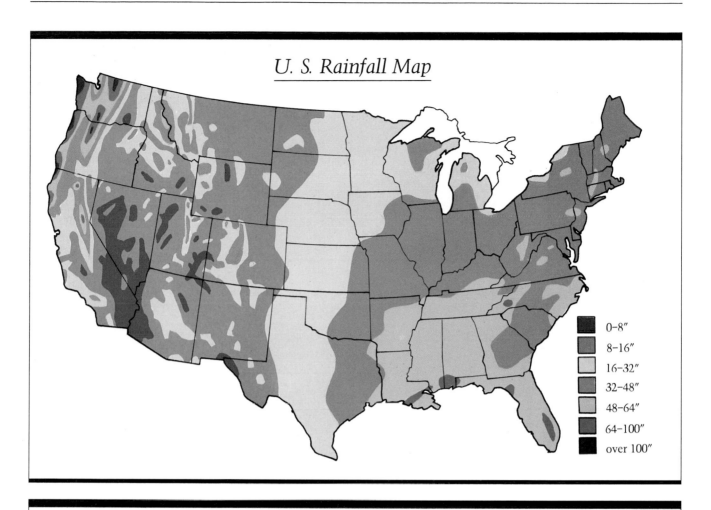

0–8"
8–16"
16–32"
32–48"
48–64"
64–100"
over 100"

U. S. Soil Map

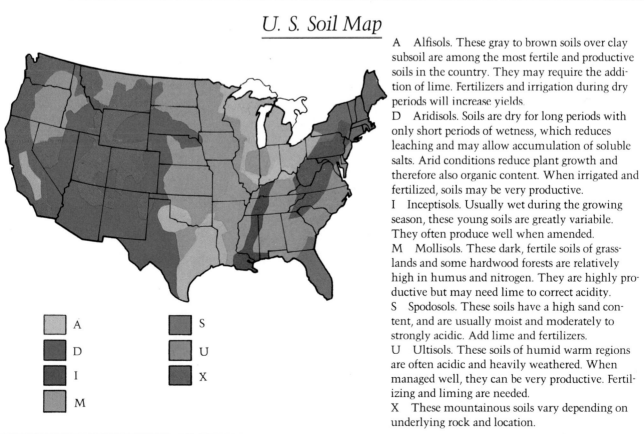

A   Alfisols
D
I
M
S
U
X

A   Alfisols. These gray to brown soils over clay subsoil are among the most fertile and productive soils in the country. They may require the addition of lime. Fertilizers and irrigation during dry periods will increase yields.

D   Aridisols. Soils are dry for long periods with only short periods of wetness, which reduces leaching and may allow accumulation of soluble salts. Arid conditions reduce plant growth and therefore also organic content. When irrigated and fertilized, soils may be very productive.

I   Inceptisols. Usually wet during the growing season, these young soils are greatly variabile. They often produce well when amended.

M   Mollisols. These dark, fertile soils of grasslands and some hardwood forests are relatively high in humus and nitrogen. They are highly productive but may need lime to correct acidity.

S   Spodosols. These soils have a high sand content, and are usually moist and moderately to strongly acidic. Add lime and fertilizers.

U   Ultisols. These soils of humid warm regions are often acidic and heavily weathered. When managed well, they can be very productive. Fertilizing and liming are needed.

X   These mountainous soils vary depending on underlying rock and location.

GLOSSARY—A GARDENER'S LANGUAGE

Acid or alkaline soil The pH of most soils is between 4.5 and 8.0. High-rainfall areas tend to have acid soils—with a pH below 6.0. Light-rainfall areas tend to have alkaline soils—with a pH above 7.0.

Amendment Any material, such as lime, compost, leaf mold, or sawdust, that is worked into the soil to improve its structure and composition. Fertilizers, although used to improve soil, usually are considered in a class by themselves.

Biodegradable Any material that decomposes readily within one year into simple elements and compounds through the action of microorganisms.

Capillary action The attraction of soil particles to water molecules, causing an upward or downward movement of the water into the soil. Simply stated, the relative pressures of water-filled pores force water into empty pores.

Chelating agent Substance added to fertilizers containing nutrients derived from metals to help keep the nutrients mobile in the soil.

Chlorosis Loss of green (chlorophyll) in leaves, especially in the tissue between leaf veining, caused by nutritional failure or disease. In severe cases, the entire leaf, except for the veins, turns yellow. Iron deficiency in azaleas is a common cause of chlorosis; the iron may be present in soils with high pH but in an insoluble form unavailable to plants. That is why acid-loving plants require a low pH for good health.

Compost A valuable soil amendment consisting almost entirely of decaying plant and animal matter.

Conservative In gardening, term applied to the practice of using natural resources wisely and sparingly.

Controlled-release fertilizers Fertilizers that release nutrients into the soil in a regulated manner. They may be slightly soluble and dissolve slowly, or plastic-coated pellets through which water penetrates slowly, freeing the soluble fertilizer.

Cover crop Also referred to as green manure, cover crops are a conservative way to improve soils and eliminate erosion in large gardens that would otherwise remain unplanted throughout the winter. Ryegrass or legumes (alfalfa, clover, cowpeas, and so forth) are sown in autumn and turned under in spring to return valuable organic matter and nitrogen to the soil.

Cultivation In a larger sense, the preparation of land for planting. In the more limited gardening sense, the loosening of soil with either hand or power tools, chiefly for the purpose of controlling weed growth.

Damping-off A plant disease caused by certain soil fungi. Seedlings either fail to emerge or die shortly after emergence. A common symptom is the rotted girdling of seedling stems at the soil line. In severe cases, older plants may be affected.

Drip line The line on the soil that represents the circumference of tree or shrub foliage; the point at which rain drips off the foliage. Note: This term should not be confused with the edge of the root zone, which often extends well beyond the drip line.

Ecology The science of the interaction of organisms and their environment.

Environment The complete surroundings of an organism or an ecological community.

Enzyme A complex protein substance produced by living cells that brings about or speeds up chemical reactions in plants and animals without itself becoming permanently altered. An enzyme is an organic catalyst.

Fallow Word applied to cropland or gardens, either cultivated or uncultivated, that remain idle and unplanted during the growing seasons.

Friable Term applied to soils that are crumbly; a desirable consistency for all garden soils.

Green manure A cover crop grown to be turned under for the purpose of improving the soil. *See* Cover crop.

Hardpan An impermeable compacted soil layer below the soil surface that may be natural or man-made. Hardpan is impenetrable to plant roots.

Heeling in A method for storing plants temporarily by burying them or covering their roots with materials such as sawdust or soil.

Humus The usually dark organic portion of the soil that is left after most organic matter has decomposed.

Impervious Not penetrable by water or other fluids.

Inorganic Refers to minerals and compounds derived from those minerals by chemical means. In the literal chemical sense, inorganic refers to compounds that lack carbon.

Ion In reference to soils, an electrically charged element or a compound either in solution or held by the electrostatic particles in the soil.

Leaching The removal of materials in solution by the passage of water down through the soil.

Loam The textural classification for soil having approximately equal amounts of sand, silt, and clay.

Microclimate The climate (prevailing atmosphere and environment) of a small area or locale; that is, a specific garden bed as opposed to the climate of that region or of the country.

Micronutrients Elements that plants need only in very small amounts.

Mulch Any material applied to soil for the purpose of reducing weeds, conserving moisture, and moderating temperature. Mulches include tree bark, wood chips, sawdust, manure, leaf mold, straw, plastic, and paper.

Organic matter Substances containing carbon compounds and usually made up of decomposed plant and animal remains. Needed in soils to maintain good structure and a healthy population of beneficial microorganisms.

Perlite A volcanic material created by heat treatment to form lightweight white granules. A common component of synthetic soils, perlite is used to lighten soils and improve drainage. Often used as a seed or rooting medium for plants.

Pesticide A material or product used to kill or control weeds, fungi, or insects.

pH A scaled logarithmic designation indicating the relative acidity or alkalinity in soils or other substances. A pH of 7.0 indicates neutrality; higher numbers indicate alkalinity and lower numbers indicate acidity.

Residual fertilizer Fertilizer left in the soil after one growing season.

Respiration As applied to plants, the chemical process by which plants take in oxygen and emit water and carbon dioxide as part of the metabolism or oxidation of plant sugars.

Saline soil A soil containing excess soluble mineral salts, including table salt (sodium chloride) and salts of calcium, magnesium, and potassium.

Scorch A condition brought about by bacteria, drought, heat, excess salts, wind, fungi, or sun exposure. Similar in appearance to the results of burning, scorch on plant foliage is characterized by yellowing or browning of plant leaves.

Side-dressing Fertilizer applied around or beside a plant so that water can carry it into the root zone.

Sodic soil Soils with a high concentration of forms of active sodium.

Species A group of plants or animals closely resembling each other that interbreed freely with each other.

Stress External factors that inhibit perfect plant growth, such as lack of water, nutrients, or light. Plant stress can be caused simply by placing the wrong plant in the wrong garden site.

Subsoil Layer of weathered soil that lies underneath the topsoil. Subsoil usually has less organic matter and poorer structure than topsoil.

Systemic In the case of pesticides, one that is absorbed into the plant's system, making the plant tissues toxic to pests.

Till To work the soil with a plow, cultivator, or other hand or power tool. Tilling soil prepares it for seeds and plants and eliminates any of the competing weeds.

Tilth Soil consistency that makes it easy to till or cultivate a garden site.

Transpiration The process by which water is emitted from plant leaves. Water is taken in by plant rootlets and rises in the plant to reach the foliage. The rate of transpiration depends upon temperature, wind, humidity, and water availability.

Variety A subgroup of plants in a species with particular like characteristics. Each variety keeps its basic character, but has at least one individual characteristic.

Vermiculite A lightweight mineral product made from mica that is expanded by heat treatment. Used as a soil additive, it lightens soil and improves drainage. A common component of synthetic soils, it's used for seeding or rooting.

Water table The level below which the ground is saturated with water.

Xeriscaping Gardening with drought-tolerant plants, a logical solution for areas prone to water shortages.

A New Mexico gardener fashioned a well-carved scarecrow that frightens all but the wood bird.

Sample Soil Test Report

Although soil test forms may differ, the results they offer are much the same. Major nutrients, soil pH, and percentage of organic matter are analyzed. Test results may also include analyses of soil texture and the electrical conductivity of soils (EC), or amount of salts in soils. Recommendations for improving the soil are given. These test results can be used as a shopping list at your local garden center. To translate the recommendations of so many pounds of nutrient per acre into specific fertilizer amounts for your garden, see page 62.

Soil Acidity

This chart shows the relationship of soil pH to plant health. The relative sweetness (basic pH) or sourness (acid pH) of the soil is what causes the nutrients so essential for plant growth to become available in soluble form or remain unavailable in compound salt form.

Extremely acid	under 4.5
Very strongly acid	4.5–4.9
Strongly acid	5.0–5.4
Medium acid	5.5–5.9
Slightly acid	6.0–6.4
Very slightly acid	6.5–6.9
Neutral	7.0–7.4
Slightly alkaline	7.5–7.9
Strongly alkaline	8.0 plus

Organic Matter

The amount of organic matter in the soil has an effect on its structure. Soils with too little organic matter are difficult to cultivate and maintain. Soils that test 3.5 or more percent organic matter will produce better plants.

Organic Matter (percent)

Low (= deficient)	0–1.0
Medium	1.0–3.5
High	3.5+

Electrical Conductivity

In arid parts of the country noted for saline soils, the electrical conductivity (EC) of saturated soil samples may be measured routinely. These tests indicate the amount of soluble salts in the soil; an excess can be damaging to plants. Results can be read as follows.

0 to 2	No damage to plants.
2 to 4	Sensitive plants may be adversely affected.
4 to 8	Many plants affected.

Soil Texture

Soil texture is described in terms of the amounts of clay, silt, and sand in the soil. For details on soil texture, see page 6. The chart below shows the composition of soil textures.

Texture	% Clay	% Silt	% Sand
Sand	0–10	0–15	85–100
Loamy sand	10–15	0–30	70–85
Sandy loam	15–20	0–50	43–84
Loam	7–27	28–50	23–52
Clay loam	27–40	15–52	20–45
Sandy clay loam	20–35	0–28	45–80
Silt loam	0–27	50–88	0–50
Silt clay loam	27–40	40–72	0–20
Sandy clay	35–55	0–20	45–65
Silty clay	40–60	40–60	0–20
Clay	40+	0–40	0–45

Soil Test Report

Recommendations for Sample:

Soil Test Information	Rating					
	Very Low	Low	Medium	High	Very High	Excess
pH						
Organic Matter						
Electrical Conductivity						
Soil Texture						
Phosphorus (P)						
Potassium (K)						
Calcium (Ca)						

Suggestions:

Soil Nutrients

The amount of major and minor nutrients present determine a soil's fertility. Tests analyze these nutrients and rate them from "very low" to "excess." When nutrients are in low supply in the soil, appropriate fertilizers should be applied at recommended levels. If nutrients are available at medium levels in the soil, the existing maintenance program should be continued. If nutrients are at high levels, there is no need to add more.

The amount of lime in a soil sample is most often given as calcium, the major element in agricultural lime. The amount of calcium in the soil relates closely to its pH level. The most important nutrient levels shown in soil tests are those for nitrogen (N), phosphorus (P), potassium (K), and calcium (Ca). Minor nutrients, commonly available in most soils, are usually not tested unless plants show problems not readily related to major nutrients.

Major Nutrients (lbs per acre)

	Nitrogen (N)	Phosphorus (P)	Potassium (K)	Calcium (Ca)	Magnesium (Mg)
Low*	0–20	0–25	0–60	0–1,000	0–100
Medium	20–50	25–50	60–120	1,000–2,500	100–250
High**	50+	50–80	120–240	2,500–4,000	250–500

Trace Nutrients (ppm)

	Copper (Cu)	Zinc (Zn)	Manganese (Mn)	Iron (Fe)
Low*	0–0.4	0–3	0–10	0–10
Medium	0.4–1.0	3–10	10–20	10–20
High**	1.0+	10+	20+	20+

* = deficient
** = sufficient

Where to Get Soil Tests

A gardener's best recourse can be the USDA Extension Service, located in the state university. The service in most states will test your soil for a nominal charge and give sound advice on cultivars and species most likely to succeed in your area. The service is not, as sometimes supposed, interested in helping only the professional grower or farmer; it is also intended to serve you, the taxpaying home gardener.

Alabama
Agricultural Experiment Station
Auburn University
Auburn, AL 36830

Alaska
Institute of Agricultural Sciences
University of Alaska
Fairbanks, AK 99701

Arizona
Agricultural Experiment Station
University of Arizona
Tucson, AZ 85721

Arkansas
Agricultural Experiment Station
University of Arkansas
Fayetteville, AR 72701

California
University-Wide Administration
Agricultural Experiment Station
University of California
Berkeley, CA 94720

Colorado
Agricultural Experiment Station
Colorado State University
Fort Collins, CO 80521

Connecticut
Agricultural Experiment Station
Box 1106
New Haven, CT 06504

Agricultural Experiment Station
University of Connecticut
Storrs, CT 06268

Delaware
Agricultural Experiment Station
University of Delaware
Newark, DE 19711

Florida
University of Florida
Institute of Food and Agricultural
Sciences
Gainesville, FL 32601

Georgia
Agricultural Experiment Station
University of Georgia
Athens, GA 30602

Hawaii
Agricultural Experiment Station
University of Hawaii
Honolulu, HI 96822

Idaho
Agricultural Experiment Station
University of Idaho
Moscow, ID 83843

Illinois
Agricultural Experiment Station
109 Mumford Hall
College of Agriculture
University of Illinois
Urbana, IL 61801

Indiana
Agricultural Experiment Station
Purdue University
West Lafayette, IN 47907

Iowa
Agricultural & Home Economics
Experiment Station
Iowa State University
Ames, IA 50010

Kansas
Agricultural Experiment Station
113 Waters Hall
Kansas State University
Manhattan, KS 66506

Kentucky
Agricultural Experiment Station
University of Kentucky
Lexington, KY 40506

Louisiana
Agricultural Experiment Station
Louisiana State University
and A & M College
Drawer E, University Station
Baton Rouge, LA 70803

Maine
Agricultural Experiment Station
105 Winslow Hall
University of Maine
Orono, ME 04473

Maryland
Agricultural Experiment Station
University of Maryland
College Park, MD 20742

Massachusetts
Agricultural Experiment Station
University of Massachusetts
Amherst, MA 01002

Michigan
Agricultural Experiment Station
Michigan State University
East Lansing, MI 48823

Minnesota
Agricultural Experiment Station
University of Minnesota
St. Paul Campus
St. Paul, MN 55101

Mississippi
Agricultural and Forestry Experiment
Station
Mississippi State University
Drawer ES
Oxford, MS 39762

Missouri
Agricultural Experiment Station
University of Missouri
Columbia, MO 65201

Montana
Agricultural Experiment Station
Montana State University
Bozeman, MT 59615

Nebraska
Agricultural Experiment Station
University of Nebraska
Lincoln, NE 68503

Nevada
Agricultural Experiment Station
University of Nevada
Reno, NV 89507

New Hampshire
Agricultural Experiment Station
University of New Hampshire
Durham, NH 03824

New Jersey
Agricultural Experiment Station
Rutgers University
Box 231
New Brunswick, NJ 08903

New Mexico
Agricultural Experiment Station
New Mexico State University
Box 3BF
Las Cruces, NM 88003

New York
Agricultural Experiment Station
Cornell University
Cornell Station, NY 14850

Agricultural Experiment Station
State Station
Geneva, NY 14456

North Carolina
Agricultural Experiment Station
North Carolina State University
Box 5847
Raleigh, NC 27607

North Dakota
Agricultural Experiment Station
North Dakota State University
State University Station
Fargo, ND 58102

Ohio
Ohio Agricultural Research
and Development Center
Ohio State University
Columbus, OH 43210

Oklahoma
Agricultural Experiment Station
Oklahoma State University
Stillwater, OK 74074

Oregon
Agricultural Experiment Station
Oregon State University
Corvallis, OR 97331

Pennsylvania
Agricultural Experiment Station
229 Agricultural Admin. Bldg.
Pennsylvania State University
University Park, PA 16802

Puerto Rico
Agricultural Experiment Station
University of Puerto Rico
Box 8
Rio Piedras, PR 00928

Rhode Island
Agricultural Experiment Station
University of Rhode Island
Kingston, RI 02881

South Carolina
Agricultural Experiment Station
Clemson University
Clemson, SC 29631

South Dakota
Agricultural Experiment Station
South Dakota State University
Brookings, SD 57006

Tennessee
Agricultural Experiment Station
University of Tennessee
Box 1071
Knoxville, TN 37901

Texas
Agricultural Experiment Station
Texas A & M University
College Station, TX 77843

Utah
Agricultural Experiment Station
Utah State University
Logan, UT 84322

Vermont
Agricultural Experiment Station
University of Vermont
Burlington, VT 05401

Virginia
Agricultural Experiment Station
Virginia Polytechnic Institute
and State University
Blacksburg, VA 24061

Virgin Islands
Agricultural Experiment Station
Box 166
College of the Virgin Islands
Kingshill, St. Croix, VI 00850

Washington
Agricultural Experiment Station
Washington State University
Pullman, WA 99163

West Virginia
Agricultural Experiment Station
West Virginia University
Morgantown, WV 26506

Wisconsin
Agricultural Experiment Station
University of Wisconsin
Madison, WI 53706

Wyoming
Agricultural Experiment Station
University of Wyoming
University Station, Box 3354
Laramie, WY 82070

Useful References For Soil Information

I n addition to the stable of gardening
books from Ortho, the following services
and publications provide useful information on soil preparation and improvement.

Brooklyn Botanic Garden Publications
Plants & Gardens handbook series (Brooklyn
Botanic Garden, 1000 Washington Avenue,
Brooklyn, NY 11225). Many of the publi-
cations include references to soils and soil
preparation.

*Soils—An Introduction to Soils and
Plant Growth*
Sixth edition, by Raymond W. Miller and
Roy L. Donahue (Prentice Hall, 1990). This
comprehensive text is a valuable resource
for students, novices, and professional
horticulturists.

USDA Extension Services
Up-to-date bulletins offering soil information
are available through the university cooper-
ative extension service in each state
(see addresses at left). Also check on availability of USDA *Yearbooks of Agriculture.*

INDEX

Note: Page numbers in bold-face type indicate principal references; page numbers in italic type refer to illustrations or photographs.

U.S. Measure and Metric Measure Conversion Chart

		Formulas for Exact Measures			Rounded Measures for Quick Reference		
	Symbol	When you know:	Multiply by:	To find:			
Mass (Weight)	oz	ounces	28.35	grams	1 oz		= 30 g
	lb	pounds	0.45	kilograms	4 oz		= 115 g
	g	grams	0.035	ounces	8 oz		= 225 g
	kg	kilograms	2.2	pounds	16 oz	= 1 lb	= 450 g
					32 oz	= 2 lb	= 900 g
					36 oz	= 2¼ lb	= 1000g (1 kg)
Volume	pt	pints	0.47	liters	1 c	= 8 oz	= 250 ml
	qt	quarts	0.95	liters	2 c (1 pt)	= 16 oz	= 500 ml
	gal	gallons	3.785	liters	4 c (1 qt)	= 32 oz	= 1 liter
	ml	milliliters	0.034	fluid ounces	4 qt (1 gal)	= 128 oz	= 3¾ liter
Length	in.	inches	2.54	centimeters	⅜ in.	= 1 cm	
	ft	feet	30.48	centimeters	1 in.	= 2.5 cm	
	yd	yards	0.9144	meters	2 in.	= 5 cm	
	mi	miles	1.609	kilometers	2½ in.	= 6.5 cm	
	km	kilometers	0.621	miles	12 in. (1 ft)	= 30 cm	
	m	meters	1.094	yards	1 yd	= 90 cm	
	cm	centimeters	0.39	inches	100 ft	= 30 m	
					1 mi	= 1.6 km	
Temperature	°F	Fahrenheit	⁵⁄₉ (after subtracting 32)	Celsius	32° F	= 0° C	
	°C	Celsius	⁹⁄₅ (then add 32)	Fahrenheit	212° F	= 100° C	
Area	in.²	square inches	6.452	square centimeters	1 in.²	= 6.5 cm²	
	ft²	square feet	929.0	square centimeters	1 ft²	= 930 cm²	
	yd²	square yards	8361.0	square centimeters	1 yd²	= 8360 cm²	
	a.	acres	0.4047	hectares	1 a.	= 4050 m²	